*How to Measure and Manage
Your Corporate Reputation*

How to Measure and Manage Your Corporate Reputation

TERRY HANNINGTON

170101

GOWER

Published by
Gower Publishing Limited
Gower House
Croft Road
Aldershot
Hants GU11 3HR
England

Gower Publishing Company
Suite 420
101 Cherry Street
Burlington, VT 05401–4405 USA

Terry Hannington has asserted his right under the Copyright, Designs and Patents Act 1988 to be identified as the author of this work.

British Library Cataloguing in Publication Data
Hannington, Terry
    How to measure and manage your corporate reputation
    1. Corporate image - Management 2. Corporations - Public
    relations
    I. Title
    659.2′85
    ISBN 0 566 08552 6

Library of Congress Cataloging-in-Publication Data
Hannington, Terry.
  How to measure and manage your corporate reputation/Terry Harrington.
     p.cm.
  Includes bibliographical references and index.
  ISBN 0-566-08552-6
  1. Corporate image. 2. Brand name products--Management. 3. Corporations--Public relations
  I. Title.
  HD59.2.H36 2003
  659.2--dc21
                                                                                    2003054704

Typeset in Stone Serif by LaserScript Ltd, Mitcham, Surrey
Printed and bound in Great Britain by MPG Books Ltd, Bodmin, Cornwall

Contents

List of figures   vii

1. Introduction   1
   Does your corporate reputation really matter?   1
   Your reputation affects business results every day of every year   2
   Reputation is a corporation's most important asset   3
   Danger signs that show you have an issue to resolve   5
   Understanding and managing reputation   6
   Who should own the issue inside your organisation   7

2. What is the Difference Between a Brand and a Reputation?   8
   Defining brand and reputation   8
   The intimate relationship between brand and reputation   10
   How a reputation is built   16
   Sage advice from an industry watcher   17

3. How is a Corporate Reputation Built Over Time?   18
   Key business events and touch-points that influence reputation   18
   In summary   26

4. 360° Mapping of Stakeholder Influence   28
   Fact-based marketing as a core principle   28
   Taking a 360° view of your reputation   29
   Building an influence map of stakeholders   33
   The list of companies and individuals who affect your reputation   34

**5. Building Executive Commitment to Measure your Reputation
   and the Key Role of Communications**   35
   Executive workshop   35
   Where should we find the resources to carry out the research – internally
      or externally?   38
   The scale and complexity of the project   39
   The role of communications in managing reputation   40

6. Researching your Organisation's Reputation   45
   Building an effective questionnaire   45
   The importance of objectivity to reveal the whole truth   46
   The nature of the interview   46
   Customer and prospect survey example   48

Surveying staff   53
Employee survey example   55
The importance of patience while the research team assesses the results 60
Including your partners in the process   60

7. The Results of your Research   61
Common issues the research may have revealed   61
Customer and staff expectation mismatch   62
Corporate messaging should be based on the real you on your best day   63
Industry analysts   63
The media   63
Customer-facing staff   65

8. Building and Implementing the Plan   71
Is the CEO leading the pack?   71
Renewing executive commitment   73
Building commitment from the middle management team   74
The importance of setting realistic expectations   76

9. Managing the Industry Analysts   77
Who are they?   77
Reactive plan   78
Proactive planning   79
Maturity required   81
Organisational issues   81

10. A Case in Point   83
Comunica   83
Stakeholders   84
Remedies   86
The bottom line   87

11. The Time to Take Action   88
The importance of continuing and renewing the plan   88
Advice on how to start a project   90
Web reputations   91
The oldest business value – reputation   92

Index   93

List of figures

1   How customers choose   4
2   The brand reputation iceberg   11
3   Monday   14
4   Touch point mapping   68
5   Performance – Reputation – Loyalty   72

1 *Introduction*

The use of the words 'corporate reputation' in the title may have evoked thoughts that this book comes from the fuzzy end of the communications industry. If that is the case, wait a moment and read a little further before passing judgement. This book contends that corporate reputations significantly affect the financial performance of commercial organisations. It advances the arguments that you can map, measure, understand and manage your reputation, thereby affecting positively your organisation's financial future.

It will discuss what you can do, practically and pragmatically, whether you are a multinational or a local player, to understand and modify your reputation. We shall examine the strategic and tactical impacts of corporate reputation, how your organisation's reputation influences business opportunities and its effect on your ability to attract the resources to capitalise on those business opportunities.

The book focuses on organisations that operate in business-to-business markets but its recommendations are relevant to all types of organisation. It presents the evidence that indicates the significance and impact of corporate reputations and discusses the importance of researching and managing it. It gives pointers to help you identify whether you have a reputation issue and who within your organisation should own the issue of its ongoing management.

It is not so difficult to accept how our personal reputations affect us in our business and private lives. Corporate reputations have an equally significant impact.

In today's world, where ideas are increasingly displacing the physical in the production of economic value, competition for reputation becomes the significant driving force, propelling our economy forward. Manufactured goods often can be evaluated before the completion of a transaction. Service providers, on the other hand, usually can offer only their reputations.

> Alan Greenspan, Harvard University commencement address,
> Cambridge, MA, USA 10 June 1999

More recently Alan Greenspan returned to the subject in a speech at New York University's Stern School of Business and stated 'Corporate reputation is fortunately re-emerging out of the ashes of the Enron debacle as a significant economic value'.

Does your corporate reputation really matter?

We have seen the impact of a reputation crisis that caused an organisation to implode and practically cease to exist in the case of Arthur Andersen. In June 2002 a jury in the United States found accountancy firm Arthur Andersen guilty of obstructing justice by shredding documents relating to the failed energy giant Enron. The verdict virtually destroyed the 89-year old organisation, once one of the world's top five accountancy firms. By this time Andersen had already lost much of its business, and two-thirds of its once 28,000 strong US workforce.

Marks & Spencer one of the world's most respected retailers was reported to have a higher reputation than the Church or the British Royal Family in a 1998 survey conducted by Corporate Edge. The research, by the brand consultancy group, asked the public to rate organisations on their willingness to listen. Marks & Spencer came top, closely followed by Body Shop and Tesco.

In May 1998 Marks & Spencer announced profits at the top end of analysts' forecasts. In the previous financial year to the end of March pre-tax profits had risen 6 per cent to £1.17 bn ($1.9 bn). However within a year the company fell on harder times with profits tumbling and rumours of takeover bids. They were forced to cut traditional links with British clothing manufacturers, close down overseas operations and rethink their brand. In November 2000 Marks & Spencer's chairman and chief executive Luc Vandevelde said there were 'no quick fixes' as sales continued to fall, and that the company, 'had lost sight of some of the basics of retailing'. The reputation of this hitherto revered retailing institution was slipping fast with its core customer base. Its latest clothing ranges had been harshly criticised by customers for being out of touch. Marks & Spencer had failed to listen effectively.

Good health was only restored when a new management team and fashion designer George Davies was recruited. Mr Davies had launched Next, one of Marks & Spencer's rivals, and designed the highly successful budget clothing range 'George' for supermarket chain Asda. His 'Per Una' styles for Marks & Spencer helped to restore sales.

Marks & Spencer had stopped to listen effectively but hopefully caught itself in time. If it had conducted appropriate research earlier to understand the changing perception of its reputation by its stakeholders, and acted upon the findings, then perhaps the story could have been far less dramatic, much more one of evolution rather than a painful revolution.

Where Marks & Spencer's sliding sales was in part a case of failing to listen to customers effectively, Andersen's questionable business practices revealed a view of the organisation that its customers and stakeholders rejected. They had engaged in behaviour that was emphatically rejected by its stakeholders. They did not want to be associated with a company that had so badly damaged its reputation.

> The purest treasure mortal times affords is spotless reputation. That away, men are but guilded loam and painted clay.
>
> William Shakespeare *Richard II*

Your reputation affects business results every day of every year

This book takes many examples from service companies but in practice reputation matters to all companies. Most companies are to a great extent service companies. They often rely on the services they are able to deliver, directly or indirectly, to complement and reinforce the effectiveness of their products. A manufacturer, for example, is not judged solely on the quality of its products but also on how well it is able to sell, service and deliver them. In the global economy product uniqueness is difficult if not impossible to achieve. Success derives from an ability to present the differentiating factors, to give your buyers a good buying experience and to be consistent in meeting your promises. The services of selling, servicing and delivering products has a tremendous impact on your success.

Irrespective of the service dimension to companies, the product itself develops a reputation over time, for performance, utility, reliability and many other qualities. Its reputation significantly affects the financial performance of the product. This book does not deal with the issue of product reputation or indeed specific service reputations but more widely with the impact of corporate reputations on future financial success.

Corporate reputation management is not only about having a good or bad reputation. It is not simply about highly public failures. Your corporate reputation affects the financial health of your organisation every day of every year. The way customers, investors, employees, suppliers, the public, analysts, media and regulators view your organisation has a profound effect on your business opportunities and your ability to attract the resources to capitalise on these opportunities. An appropriate reputation helps you to win new business, retain existing customers, attract new employees, gain favourable media coverage and acts as a barrier against competitors.

Let us put aside global rankings of corporate reputations like the one conducted by the Reputation Institute.[†] Consider instead the concept of having an appropriate reputation.

- What is your corporate reputation?
- Is it helping or hindering you?
- Is your reputation, in this sector of your activity, appropriate for you to achieve your corporate ambitions?

These are the questions we need to ask and find sound answers for.

Reputation is a corporation's most important asset

Executives often talk about brand but very few mention reputation and even fewer believe they should spend time assessing that reputation and actively managing it. The contention of this book is that you should map, measure and understand your reputation. Once measured and understood you can take concrete actions to minimise the negative and capitalise on the positive affects.

In most organisations, management attempts to protect tangible assets which range from proprietary designs to trade secrets, even office furniture and fixtures. Yet they often fail to protect their organisation's best asset, its reputation, with equal vigour.

It is difficult to place an accurate value on an organisation's reputation. A crude but viable estimate is the current market value of the company minus the tangible assets. By sub-contraction you arrive at an estimated current valuation of your reputation. Does it look like it is an asset worth protecting and managing now?

RESEARCH EVIDENCE

Research into the factors affecting the selection of companies to be invited to bid for business-to-business contracts highlights the issue of reputation as a highly significant selection factor. The final choice of supplier is also strongly influenced by the buyer's perception of the supplier's reputation.

One source of research into this area is ITSMA, an American organisation that focuses on advising IT services marketers. ITSMA has carried out research over a number of years, as part of their service to members, attempting to understand what influences decision makers when deciding who to invite to bid for contracts and what influences their final choice of vendor. When selecting whom to invite to bid for contracts, buyers quote their prior relationship with the vendor, a seminar or workshop and recommendations from their peers as their most favoured sources of information. It seems that in this age of sophisticated marketing and electronic information sources word of mouth still has great potency.

Figure 1 is one of a number of research findings that point to reputation as being the highest ranked influencer. ITSMA asked the question 'How influential were the following in helping you make your decision to purchase services from your vendor?' The results, shown in the figure, are consistent with ITSMA's findings over a number of years.

The most important influencers were shown to be an overall assessment of the vendor's reputation, impressions gained via seminars or workshops, peer recommendations, vendor's sales staff and personal experience. These should not come as a surprise to us. Business-to-business relationships have always been based on trust and more specifically the trust between key representatives of the buyer and seller. Reputation in effect expresses the qualities of the trust you have been awarded by your stakeholders. This emphasis on trust seems to be even more important for the service sector where the 'product' is less physically tangible. Selecting a service provider is a potentially reputation-damaging activity for the person or group charged with making the decision. Any failure of service by the selected service provider is often highly visible within their organisations. They need to be convinced and very comfortable with their chosen selection.

For business-to-consumer markets, trust in the key representatives of the organisation is replaced, in many cases, by trust in the brand that stands as a symbol for the organisation. In

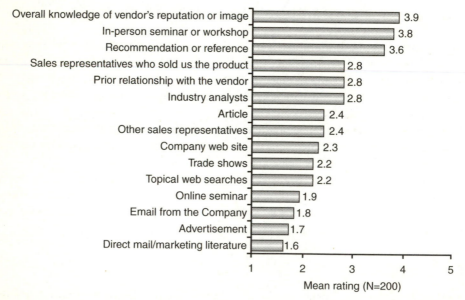

Figure 1   How customers choose

Note: Mean ratings based on a 5-point scale in which 1 = not at all influential and 5 = very influential

Source: ITSMA, *How Customers Choose Survey, 2002*

some instances the CEO embodies and expresses the values of the organisation and becomes the most recognised symbol, as is the case with Richard Branson and Virgin.

ANECDOTAL EVIDENCE

When I meet the senior executives from the major customers of the organisations I work with, I always try to ask the question 'Why did you do business with us?' The most often quoted response is 'I felt comfortable with your people' or 'I felt I could trust you'. I am always surprised by this level of candour admitting to the emotional nature of the decision. I can remember only a very few occasions when, for example, price or technical competence was the mentioned factor. Nevertheless, if your technical competence or price does not meet the accepted norms of your market then of course emotional factors will not sway the decision. In most cases you are in a competitive situation with a number of suppliers who are all well qualified to provide the required product or service. The winners are, more often than not, those companies that have the right kind of relationship with the buyers and are able to reassure buyers that they will deliver what they have promised.

Reputation is a corporation's most important asset. Strong and durable reputations are built over time by doing the 'right things right' across the organization, and taking appropriate credit for achievements. Reputation influences all the goals a corporation can set – getting a higher stock multiple, generating higher profit margins, attracting and retaining the best employees, finding strong business partners, and capturing both the attention and loyalty of customers. Reputation also is a critical factor in how well an organization weathers a crisis.

Bill Pendergast, Corporate Reputation Management Chairman
Fleishman-Hillard, Washington D.C. USA

Danger signs that show you have an issue to resolve

It is easy to be critical about the lack of attention paid to reputation. There are probably multiple reasons for this: some organisations have been blinded by brand awareness concerns; in other organisations key management have been insulated from the realities of the organisation's reputation; and in some cases 'Yes men' surround senior executives. In their desire to climb the corporate ladder they are very adept at telling us what they think we want to hear. It is no surprise that insulated business executives are often shocked when the media attacks their organisation or when they fail to print every one of their important words. Even within more 'in-touch' organisations it is tough to accept criticism, even constructive criticism, from your stakeholders and hence easier to avoid it.

SYMPTOMS OF A CORPORATE REPUTATION ISSUE

The following list of symptoms is based on one developed by Elliot S. Schreiber, Industry Professor at the Michael G. DeGroote School of Business at McMaster University in Canada. It seems to hit the mark as a litmus test for danger signs to look for. Consider your own organisation honestly and objectively: how would you answer the following questions?

- Despite all of your communications and marketing claims of product, service or corporate superiority, does the market still seem to be unclear about your organisation and its value proposition?
- Are you losing market share?
- Have your bid-to-win ratios deteriorated over time?
- Do your executives underestimate the impact new competitors may have on your organisation's market position?
- Have you found that executives and staff in the organisation do not fully understand what your customers want in terms of products and services?
- Is your corporate positioning based on a snappy slogan or tag line rather than a real differentiation?
- Is a large proportion of your available spending directed into advertising to 'raise awareness'?
- Does your management think that the higher reputation enjoyed by your competitors is largely the result of their more effective PR or advertising?
- Does management accuse editors, analysts or other media of bias when dealing with your organisation's news?
- Are proposals for new ways of working or thinking about the way you address your chosen markets met with comments such as: 'we tried that years ago and it didn't work', or 'if it's not broken, don't fix it', or 'let's just focus on today's business'?

If you answered yes to some of the questions above then read the rest of this book and act on it. It may well give you the highest ROI of any other single item in today's 'to do' list.

Understanding and managing reputation

The core contention of this book is that you should map the key stakeholders who are the influencers of your reputation. Your stakeholders are your customers, prospects, employees, industry analysts, financial analysts, the media, partners and regulatory authorities. When you think you understand who is in each group of organisations and individuals, map each group's relative importance and influence over other groups. The process continues with research on selected groups to measure and understand what your reputation really is in their eyes. And finally you should implement a programme to manage reputation on an ongoing basis.

It is not enough to make assumptions or take what limited anecdotal evidence you may have today as comfort that you do not have an issue. You need to know the facts. You may already have data from market research, customer satisfaction surveys and brand studies. But beware: these surveys were designed to meet specific objectives and the data is unlikely to have been collected in a consistent manner across a number of stakeholder groups. The information we need is from a wide circle of stakeholders to help us understand not only what they feel about us but the way each group influences the other. This objective demands a different set of questions.

A reputation research and management programme allows you to fine tune your delivery and levels of customer comfort, helps remove barriers to new business opportunities and ensures you are able to maximise your current potential. It discloses areas of weakness in your delivery of services and products to your customers. It reveals issues of poor or confusing communications. It identifies issues of staff knowledge deficiencies. It uncovers morale and motivational problems.

But any marketer worth their salt knows fulfilling today's needs will not of itself ensure an organisation's longevity. The understanding and fulfilment of the potential customer's unrealised needs is the key to that door. Research carried out as part of a reputation management programme may give you some pointers to these unrealised needs but only as a by-product not as a main intent.

Who should own the issue inside your organisation

In most cases the logical owner would be the marketing group. Their role is to represent the customer and other external stakeholders within your organisation. They should be aware of and tracking evolving market demands. They usually have some responsibility for internal and external communications. However in many organisations the media are managed by a corporate communications group, financial analysts by the chief financial officer and of course staff issues by the human relations team. To make things even more complicated the marketing function may be organised by business unit or product or service offering.

The market or divisional split is not a significant issue as you can work very effectively within these boundaries to understand your reputation and its impact on your divisional performance. However, to understand your reputation fully you need to survey all the stakeholder groups, so you may find you meet some demarcation issues when you seek to research stakeholders outside of your domain. The findings of this research may demand changes to processes, messaging, training or even staff. This type of organisational change will require all the key groups within the organisation to play their role. Therefore, projects that are sponsored by the CEO, the Marketing Director or other directors at senior management team level have the highest probability of success.

† The Reputation Institute is a private research organisation founded by Charles Loubrun, Professor Emeritus at the Stern School of Business, New York, and Cees van Riel, Professor of Business and Society at Rotterdam School of Management, Erasmus University.

2 What is the Difference Between a Brand and a Reputation?

Let us try to define some terms before we go much further otherwise I will fall into the trap of leaving my most important stakeholder, you the reader, behind in bewilderment. Over the last few years corporate brands and reputation have been lumped together as one entity in the minds of many executives. Let us try to make pragmatic differentiations between these concepts. The definitions discussed below focus on corporate brands and reputations in primarily, but not exclusively, business-to-business situations.

We will also discuss how brand and reputation interact and the ways many organisations view this issue. They can often be blinded by brand and fail to see the relevancy and role of reputation.

Defining brand and reputation

WHAT IS A CORPORATE REPUTATION?

The key differentiation between brand and reputation is that reputation is created by responses to a set of questions the answers to which define the qualities of the organisation. Brand, however, is very much linked to your reaction to a visual symbol. Reputation is defined by the responses to the types of questions stakeholders ask about a company to form their perception of the organisation. It is the answers to specific questions such as those contained in the list below which are grouped for convenience by subject:

- **Products and services**
  Will they stand behind their products and services?
  Are they innovative?
  Do they provide high quality products and services?
  Are their products and services good value for the money?

- **Financial performance**
  Do they have a strong financial record?
  Are they a low-risk investment?
  Do they have strong prospects for future growth?
  Do they tend to out-perform their competitors?

- **Vision and leadership**

  Do they have excellent leaders?

  Do they have a clear vision of their future?

  Do they usually recognise and take advantage of market opportunities?

- **Working environment**

  Is it well managed?

  Are they a good organisation to work for?

  Do they have good employees?

- **Social responsibility**

  Do they support good causes?

  Are they an environmentally responsible organisation?

  Do they maintain high standards in the way they treat people?

- **Emotional appeal**

  Do you have a good feeling about the organisation?

  Do you respect the organisation?

  Do you trust the organisation?

- **Sector specific**

  Do they provide suitable solutions?

  Have they a track record of successful projects?

  Do they have the right people and processes for this type of project?

The above list is based on the Harris-Fombrun Reputation Quotient which uses twenty questions to measure six dimensions of reputation.

Reputation is the attitudes and feelings to the specific qualities of the organisation. It is an assessment of the performance of an organisation's products, services, activities and employees. It may well vary from market sector to market sector if the organisation operates in multiple markets. It is the current opinions of a group of people who have some form of relationship with the organisation. A corporate reputation is a perception of an organisation's ability to meet the expectations of its stakeholders. It describes the rational and emotional attachments that they form with the organisation.

WHAT IS A BRAND?

Laurie Young Global Head of Marketing for PwC's Corporate Finance and Recovery Division and PwC Brand Advisor believes that brand is 'an entity that is loved so much that people are prepared to pay more for it than the material benefit obtained'. Laurie argues that there is a continuum that starts with awareness of what he calls 'fame' and ends with 'brand', with 'reputation' lying half way between the two. He believes you get to be a 'brand' by the passage of time and it is built by your reputation.

Successful brands certainly give consumer-focused companies higher street prices or higher sales volumes. The evidence is visible each time you visit your local supermarket or high street. Whether this is equally true of business-to-business transactions is less obvious. In this arena very few organisations have achieved brand status using Laurie's definition. McKinsey may be one that has achieved this. It has consistently reported higher revenue per consultant figures than other similar consultancies. IBM Global Services seems to be on the way to building a highly credible reputation and research has shown it is the most widely recognised information technology service brand in the United States.

I largely agree with Laurie's analysis but I would tend to view brand and reputation more as two complimentary entities. They merge into one another and making a precise division between them is neither necessary nor useful. In my view a brand is: *A visual symbol that represents an organisation or product.* In essence that is all that a brand is. However, we know that over time this visual symbol becomes attached to an abbreviated set of emotions. We can all quote examples of symbols and our attached emotions. These emotions are highly personal and not necessarily the ones you are intended to feel by the owners of the brand. Let's look at a few examples.

- Gucci – Expensive and glamorous.
- Versace – Expensive and vulgar
- Marks & Spencer – Middle of the road, reliable quality, unadventurous
- IBM – Solid, reliable and professional

We could choose many more to consider and I do not expect you to necessarily agree with my highly personal reactions to these symbols. The brand owner may try to mould our reaction towards their brand, but human nature being what it is, our response may be more influenced by factors other than advertising or promotional activities. I believe, as Laurie Young, that reputation contributes largely to building the brand with the passage of time. Widespread recognition amplifies the effects and in some cases the brand name becomes so well associated it is absorbed into the language, as is the case of say Hoover, which has become a verb. However, Hoover seems to have kept its brand recognition but lost its reputation with its consumers who largely prefer other vacuum cleaners.

The key quality of brand is that you recognise it and it has some values attached to it. In effect it acts as a decision shortcut to quote Harry Beckwith in *Selling the Invisible*. In both cases both brand and reputation are predictors of future behaviour for consumers. Corporate brands at a high level of generalisation but reputation is much more granular and case specific. If the emotions attached to the brand are positive and appropriate then this obviously helps in a process of selecting an organisation or product. If the brand is widely recognised, equally, this multiplies its positive effects. In business-to-business having a recognised name helps. It reassures less informed parties involved in the decision process that a reliable organisation has been selected

The issue of a brand's impact in business-to-business markets leads to many questions. How many effective brands can you have in each market space? Does the brand element cease to be a differentiator in a crowded market? Is a business-to-business market genuinely brand sensitive? I suspect that while we could spend time trying to answer these questions, effort invested in understanding your organisations' reputation will give you a far higher payback.

The intimate relationship between brand and reputation

Brand is the visual tip of an iceberg raised above the waterline as a symbol of the organisation, its products and services. Reputation lurks below the surface. The highly visible brand elements have their role in forming our attitudes. The extent of that role depends on the significance of other influences we are exposed to. In consumer products they may be very influential. Advertising, the visual style of the product and the way that it is promoted, displayed and sold will shape a large part of our reaction to it. Combined with these elements is our use of the product and influences from other stakeholders. This total spectrum of influences forms our perception of its reputation. Reputation supports the development of a positively recognised brand or prevents it if that reputation is inappropriate. A successful brand is a brand with a widely recognised positive and appropriate reputation. The brand becomes attached to an abbreviated set of emotions that is widely shared. In Laurie Young's words it has become sufficiently loved to justify a higher price than similar competitive products.

In business-to-business markets, for any size of organisation, the highly visible elements of the brand diminish in importance as the available influences are much greater in the below the waterline area of reputation. Even when you consider local retailers or restaurants, the mix of influences that build the reputation of these organisations lie very much below the waterline. Their reputations are created by the comments of friends and contacts, press mentions, and personal experience. Advertising is usually not effective in building a reputation in this instance. It may be a useful trigger for the reputation questions but it is not in itself a reputation builder. The most influential, least visible and greater part of the iceberg lies in wait ready to trap negligent management who fail to take account of its influence on their corporate futures.

The reputation of an organisation and its people, in the eyes of its stakeholders, is built over time to a great extent by infectious history. Assessments of the organisation's past performance, opinions and valuations are passed from person to person and via the media. They build a complex web of reputation influences that is decisive on the development of a positively recognised brand.

Irrespective of its influence on brand development, reputation affects your organisation's ability to attract and retain business opportunities and the resource to capitalise on them every day, every week, every year.

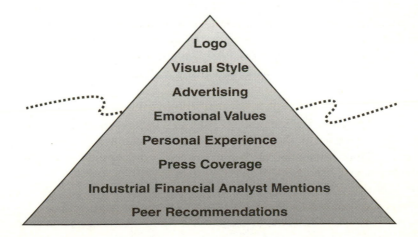

Figure 2   The brand reputation iceberg

HOW DOES THE BUSINESS WORLD OFTEN VIEW THIS RELATIONSHIP?

Whenever I have discussed the issue of brand and reputation with business leaders many of them place brand and reputation in a single large pot. If you talked about debt-to-equity ratios, cash flow, gross margin, EBIT (Earnings before Interest and Tax) and EBITDA (Earnings before Interest, Tax and Depreciation) as simply 'book keeping' they would probably take you to task for being guilty of naive thinking. But the same business leaders will often consign the complex issues of how the business is perceived to an equally woolly part of the corporate mind.

When you discuss reputation with the PR community they normally restrict their definition of reputation to that of how an organisation is viewed by the media. While they are effusive about the impact of reputation their view of it is rather narrow.

The branding communities have developed complex definitions and dictionaries to define their views of the impact of brands. Landor publishes on its web site a 'proprietary' lexicon of phrases to define branding terms with definitions such as:

- Brand – The sum of all the characteristics, tangible and intangible, that make the offer unique.
- Brand equity – The value of the brand in its holistic sense to its owners as a corporate asset.
- Brand essence – The distillation of a brand's intrinsic characteristics into a succinct core concept.

Other brand warriors talk of 'the brand experience'. But they usually do not include the value of one the oldest corporate and human values, reputation, within their branding dictionaries. These groups are enthusiastically practising some classic marketing techniques. They have defined an issue and named it, created a proprietary system of language to describe it, and attempted to get this accepted as the standard definitions. Thereby they hope to become the intellectual owners of this issue. However, while this usefully brings clarity and sharpness to the issues, we all need to recognise that if you extend too far with the minutiae of your definitions and claims of importance you may move beyond the credibility limits of your stakeholders.

I believe the reputations of companies such as IBM and Fujitsu, who operate in global markets, cannot adequately be covered by the concept of brand alone. They have a complex set of products and services. They operate in a bewildering range of markets. Their reputations will differ in substance from market to market and even from product to product within those markets. Stakeholders in Malaysia will not feel the same as those in Denmark. The personal computer purchaser may have a very different view from the global services customer.

Smaller companies that operate in one market with a much more limited set of offerings may have reputations that differ from stakeholder to stakeholder group and market segment to market segment. Even if they operate in one geographical area with one product, reputation is highly influential on future success. Understanding the differences of reputation between geographies, markets or products is of course very useful. These differences tell us it is not enough to know your global brand status. This is a small and relatively superficial part of the picture. The most significant issue is the specific impact of your reputation, in specific markets or geographies. These shades of reputation have a daily impact on your business opportunities.

The fundamental issue is to understand and manage the effects stakeholders' views have on your organisation for a specific product or service sector or geography. Understanding and managing reputation can help an organisation generate and retain business opportunities by lowering previously unseen barriers.

I believe that viewing the issue of the way stakeholders feel about an organisation with jargon or proprietary definitions can restrict the ability of the whole organisation to understand the issues. The understanding and management of the way stakeholders view your organisation, be it generically or in relation to a specific geography or product, is a whole company issue – whole in the sense that it affects all the groups and departments within the organisation. Responding to the challenges that research into your reputation may bring is a whole company challenge. Defining an issue in a way that may only be understood by marketing groups causes the language used to contain and restrict understanding. Many groups within the organisation need to be aware and involved. The language used to describe the issues should facilitate a wider understanding of how your company satisfies the expectations of all your stakeholders and what they think about you.

CORPORATE ENTHUSIASM FOR BRAND

When you consider corporate behaviour in recent years a great deal of attention has been focused on brand. During the 'dot.com' bubble venture capital was lavishly spent on advertising trying to build brand awareness and values even before these organisations had started to deliver anything of significance to customers. The wreckage of the dot.com era has left behind very few companies who have managed to build viable businesses and reputations through the delivery of real consistent value to customers.

The large consultancy companies have led the way in trying to establish recognised brands and even to appear not to be consultants at all. Their motivation is obvious after the collapse of Arthur Andersen. 'A lot of corporate failures have been laid at the door of consultancies', says Helen Blake Marketing Director of Cap Gemini Ernst & Young. Fortunately for Andersen Consulting they were forced to re-brand and become Accenture well before the industry started to fall apart. In a hugely costly, but largely successful, exercise they have distanced themselves from their Andersen roots. Accenture developed a five-year plan with a budget running into many hundreds of millions of dollars with the objective of evolving their brand and firmly establishing themselves as leading players in the technology service marketplace.

Not all attempts have been as successful. PriceWaterhouseCoopers Consulting decided to call itself 'Monday'. This was greeted by many bewildered comments and derision from the media. Monday was sold to IBM a few months later and the name disappeared.

Alan Rattray, Marketing director of Landor (the agency that created the Accenture brand), said of the consultancies, 'It's no longer enough just to be a part of the magic circle of elite firms; they are not selling services any more but reputation.' Service companies have always sold reputation if ITSMA's research is to be believed and only just now are the brand wizards starting to acknowledge its vital role.

The IT sector is not alone in trying a Superman 'with one bound he was free' re-branding strategy. Consignia, the new name for the British Post Office, attracted heavy criticism when the new brand was established in March 2001. At the time the Post Office was incorporated as a public limited company. The BBC web site published many user views about the new name for the organisation. The following two comments are typical of the responses.

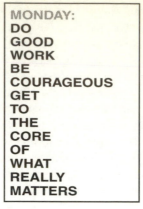

MONDAY:
DO
GOOD
WORK
BE
COURAGEOUS
GET
TO
THE
CORE
OF
WHAT
REALLY
MATTERS

Figure 3   Monday

Does it really make any difference? There was so much made of the name 'Consignia' that it was as well known as Royal Mail. The name means nothing, they need a kick up the backside!

Ian, England

It may have been the worst year in financial terms for the Post Office, but in terms of performance we have seen month on month improvements in the service this year. Give the name Consignia a chance. I agree, it was a waste of money, but don't throw good money after bad changing it again!

Simon Cooper, UK

However, on 4 November 2002 they did indeed change their name again, to the Royal Mail Group. When you change something as familiar and widely known as the name of the Post Office the risks are high; it disturbs the emotions attached to the old brand name and forces us to rearrange our familiar associations. If there is no perceived benefit for this disruption then anger is often the response.

Midland Bank, prior to being acquired by HSBC, tried to change its reputation by an advertising campaign styling itself as 'the listening bank'. The press pilloried them after instances of strongly worded letters being sent to customers with overdrafts. Unfortunately some of the recipients had recently died and their relatives reacted very badly to this uncaring communication.

A focus on trying to build brands marks the recognition that the selection process for business-to-business contracts is complex and the extent of influence by soft emotional factors in the decision process is higher than most people would care to admit.

In the sector of business-to-consumer the relevance of brand as a driver of repeat purchase, usually at higher prices than less well regarded brands, is indisputable.

The investment analyst community have started to recognise the impact a strong brand can have on future earnings and hence share values. Research carried out in 2001 by Brand Finance showed that 76 per cent of the investment analysts they surveyed wanted more information on brand values in annual reports. The same survey showed that 77 per cent believe branding will become more important in the next five years.

Their desire to be able to place a value on brand can be traced to the Financial Reporting Standard 10 & 11 – the current accounting standards relating to brands in the UK, while IAS38 is the International equivalent. FRS 10 & 11 oblige companies to capitalise acquired goodwill and intangible assets. However, internally generated assets are not permitted on the balance sheet, so for example Diageo can capitalise acquired brands such as Smirnoff but not organic grown brands such as Baileys, though both may be of equal value.

In markets such as drinks and clothes the emotional aspects of the brand have tremendous value. Walking along the supermarket shelves selecting Smirnoff over another unknown brand is a low risk choice for which you pay a penalty of only a small amount of money. Buying Armani or Gucci will cost you more but the label gives you a warm glow of having arrived in the affluent set. Human nature being what it is, we are frail and need the support of symbols to garner the approval of our friends and peers and to show the world we are successful. The relationship with the product may be brief and superficial. As long as it does not fall apart quickly or taste disgusting the price you pay is for the cachet, not the utility. Of course a brand's value and emotional attachments would not usually be created in the first place if they did produce inferior quality products.

BRAND MAY NOT BE EVERYTHING IT IS BELIEVED TO BE

Anthony Miller, IT industry analyst of Ovum Holway, comments that he is 'highly cynical about brand and very hot on reputation, because recurring revenue streams and profitability are the real measures of success and only achieved by continuing to meet product and service promises'.

If we move from products with which you have a superficial relationship to one that could seriously impact your future as a manager, or indeed your organisation's future, then the game changes. It is dangerous to assume that the same rules apply as in consumer markets. So this is where your reputation starts to play very seriously in the game. Even if you have a well-known and respected brand it may not help you to extend into new areas of your market space or even to be successful in the long term in your core market.

One of the most successful and certainly the largest IT services player today is IBM with IBM Global Services, but in the mid-1990s IBM realised that despite being probably the largest player in the IT services market it did not have a reputation for service. Its customers when asked if they would consider IBM for service contracts said, 'We did not realise IBM was in the service business'. IBM discovered via research that it was probably losing four out of five opportunities even within its own customer base.

Microsoft has admitted that despite having a very strong and recognised brand their push to provide high criticality services to the corporate market, in conjunction with their partners, was tough going. They were not considered to be credible and committed. They just did not have a reputation for service.

Logica in the UK felt it had some problems in their government business sector. They commissioned an external organisation to find out what was the reality of their reputation in this important part of their business. What they found worried them deeply. The essence of the comments from their customers can be paraphrased as

Well you do a good technical job and you are overall quite efficient. But when your people come on site they do not mix with our staff. There is no knowledge transfer or social interaction. When you have finished the project and we would like to discuss future developments instead of a conversation you take the bull by the horns, produce a bid and pester us until we sign it. If we could find another provider I think we would.

In each of these cases we have a reputation issue not a brand issue. They had risked floundering on the nine tenths of the iceberg buried below the waterline, the reputation factor. In each of these cases the respective companies understood they had a problem, they took actions to research and manage the issue and were largely successful.

How a reputation is built

Reputation is the product of infectious history. It reflects the reactions of people to how you have behaved. Reputation is built from first-hand experience with your product or service and from the referred experience of others. Reputation is articulated and granular. It is the response to a set of questions and measures the ability to satisfy your stakeholders' requirements. It is a predictor of future behaviour.

Microsoft has a high level of brand recognition but not a reputation for service. Logica was ostensibly doing a great job but leaving its customers not completely satisfied. IBM did not have a reputation for service despite it being one of the largest players in the marketplace.

Microsoft responded by creating a separate profit centre for service instead of the previous cost centre and redoubling its efforts to be seen as a committed service provider.

Logica changed its account management practices to try to modify the unhelpful elements of its reputation.

IBM's reaction was to spend 74 million dollars in the next couple of years to create recognition for the name of IBM Global Services. They have succeeded and in recent studies they have become the most well-known IT service provider. They have built a solid reputation over the last five years as a highly competent service organisation. A great deal of this success can be laid at the feet of Lou Gerstner and his belief in marketing honed by his experience in Nabisco, American Express and McKinsey. He recruited marketers from outside of the IT industry to drive the building of a services reputation for IBM. These new-style marketers instilled a culture of fact-based marketing, which, as apposed to opinion-based marketing, relies on solid research and data as the foundation for making decisions.

IBM's fact-based marketing is drawn from the consumer sector where a statistical analysis of customer and market feelings and requirements is a more normal procedure. In the business-to-business market key representatives of the provider usually know personally senior figures of major customers. Social and other events provide good opportunities to talk directly to key decision makers. From this you may feel you understand your customers and know what they feel about you. However this can be a dangerous illusion as one senior IBM executive told me, 'they drink my wine and do business with somebody else behind our backs'.

Reputation is a powerful force that can make or break your organisation as Anderson has found to its cost. But on a less dramatic level the reputation you hold within the markets and business sectors you operate in will have a significant effect on the future success of your organisation. But it may not be an easy decision to invest in understanding your reputation. When did you last ask somebody what he or she really feels about you? The emotional barriers to asking the big question are high. Human nature is to avoid asking and assume that you have a positive and appropriate reputation. But all the evidence I have seen tells me that the results of research, into the reputation you hold with your stakeholders, changes the way you conduct business in the future. It always highlights 'could do better' issues that are holding your organisation back today.

In my experience objectively researched data about your reputation, rather than opinions about opinions, is a far more reliable way to understand the issue and then have the confidence to act upon the findings.

Sage advice from an industry watcher

Julie Schwartz, ITSMA's Vice President of Research, has spent many years researching the services marketplace not only with ITSMA but also with State Street Research, which provides investor analysis on technology companies for corporate clients. Earlier in her career Julie also was Director of Professional Services Research for Dataquest and Manager of Research for the Ledgeway Group.

Julie believes 'If you have some money to spend then spend it on your customer relationship development and reputation building. You will obtain a much better return. Only think about advertising if you are prepared for the long haul and you have a lot of money to spend.'

3 How is a Corporate Reputation Built Over Time?

 Just walk into a room and without even opening your mouth you will have already started to build a reputation, even if nobody in the room has met you before.

Key business events and touch-points that influence reputation

Every way that your organisation touches your key stakeholders will build its reputation, for better or for worse. But some of these interactions will hold the potential for a greater impact on your reputation than others. The key to understanding these critical touch-points is to understand that reputation is a collection of emotions peppered with a few facts. The critical touch-points will be those that affect the recipient's emotions in the most profound way. Understand these critical touch-points and we will be well along the track of avoiding some of the more obvious ways of developing a less than positive reputation.

Let's consider some of the high profile touch-points that may have affected your reputation.

BIDDING FOR NEW CONTRACTS

For a corporate buyer the process of selecting organisations to bid for contracts starts with a list of potential suppliers drawn from the buyer's experience, recommendations from peers or perhaps industry analysts. Usually a group of individuals is gathered together rather than one person to constitute the buying team. On many occasions the first step in the process will be a request for information (RFI) that asks the suppliers to prove their suitability to bid. Care in managing this part of the process is critical. Too much or too little information and activity can be equally damaging to the level of comfort the buyer has with the potential supplier. A written response that does not consider the individual situation of the potential customer's organisation can show a 'not really interested' attitude. You may be invited to present your organisation in the flesh and again the same cautions apply, too little or too much are both highly risky. Too little attention to giving a presentation that talks to the individual situation or industry of the buyer again shows lack of attention and perhaps even arrogance. Bringing a large entourage and presenting beyond the allotted time leaving little room for buyer questions can be seen as an insecure response. For the buyer a successful bid process is critical. A great deal of effort will have been expended in building the bidders list, outlining the bid requirements, and indeed may have been put into obtaining project approval in the first place. There are many ways the buyer's emotions can be compromised in this early stage of a bid process. For the potential bidder you want to be on the short list but you also want to be sure you leave the buyer with a wholly positive view of your organisation. Already you have been selected by the buyer and as such you have a responsibility to ensure their choice is justified if you want to avoid them feeling let down by you.

In any competitive bidding process it is important to have the last word if you can. Memories are short and what you heard last is always the freshest in your mind. But avoid the danger of having nothing to say in those last words other than to recap on what you have already said. That implies your audience did not listen to you and may have forgotten what you said. It is true of course but telling them this, by implication, is neither helpful nor flattering. Use the last word to give, for instance, a recent reference to a satisfied user of your product or services. This a veritable parcel of pre-packed reputation ready to prove your reliability and competence, very powerful stuff. The best sort of last word is to choose one of your best arguments for this last opportunity to make your point. I like to call this *a slow burner* – that is an idea that sits in the buyer's mind and is not easy to reject. Usually the most successful are those that appeal to base emotions such as fear of loss. Leaving the room after having subtly reminded the buyer you are the safest choice, either personally or corporately, is a powerful place to be.

The final bidders list will be arrived at after the RFI submissions are considered. Then the more detailed bid process is likely to begin. Depending on the size and type of contract this process can take a few weeks or many months. It provides many excellent opportunities to build a positive relationship and reputation with the buyer whether you win this contract or not.

The next step will be for the buyer to issue a request for tender (RFT) to those organisations they have selected to bid. The terminology for such documents will vary from industry to industry but I am sure you understand the differing intentions of an RFI and a RFT. An RFI requests information from which to select a list of bidders and demands more generic information to qualify the bidders. An RFT seeks a specific response to a specific requirement with the intention to conclude a contract with one of the bidders.

The bid response document should be highly professional. It needs to allow the buyer to see your responses to the questions asked in the RFT. The document must answer all the questions as fully as is necessary for clarity. To produce a document that does not respond to the questions asked or does not do so fully is dangerous. From personal experience, many buyers I spoke to, after the bidding stage was closed, complained about other bidders who had not submitted acceptable responses either because they did not answer the questions posed or did not answer fully enough. The emotions of the buyers were ones of considerable annoyance; their voices would become emphatic when they talked about it and you could feel the strength of the underlying emotions. They felt the organisations that had produced the poor bid documents neither wanted to win the business and had rejected the buyer and his company. Rejection is always tough to handle.

During the bid response process emotions on the side of your bid team will be running high and they can easily fail to pay full attention to the feelings of the potential customer's bid team as their competitive spirits takes over. Having a good bid management process in which someone is focusing closely on the individuals in the buyer's team and how they are reacting to your behaviour and messages can go a long way to avoiding both losing a deal and a potential customer.

The person charged with approving bids should also be asking questions not simply about the profitability and technical soundness of your proposal but also about the level of care being paid to both the bid process and the personalities involved. Irrespective of the size and scope of the bid and the size of your organisation bidding is an expensive and time-consuming process. Improving your win rate by paying great care to selecting and managing bids tightly is essential. I have met many sales forces with low win rates and highly expensive sales costs because insufficient control was exercised over bid selection and management. It is often better to decline to bid gracefully where the bid is assessed to have a low probability of success. But when you decide not to bid great care must be taken to explain the reasons to your potential customer. Even if the answer is that you are so involved with many other bids that you cannot do this one the justice it deserves.

Sales teams that try to bid for every opportunity generally pay poor attention to them all. The resulting low win rates soon drive them to become dispirited and even more desperate. It is a downward spiral that you need to stop by firm action to implement internal bid management processes that ensure you invest your efforts in higher probability or strategically critical bids.

Badly formed bids and repeated losses build you a reputation as a loser organisation and that is something we must try to avoid. Hoping that you might just win this one, despite the high odds against you, is the same emotion that keeps casinos in business.

CONTRACT FULFILMENT

Hopefully you win the contract and of course you have to deliver what you promised. However a degree of expectation management may be necessary. It is better to promise less than you actually deliver rather than the other way around. It is better to admit that you may have some problems in the early phase of a contract or the installation of a new product as the staff, on both sides, become used to the individual demands of the contract or the equipment is tuned. If the contract has been moved from one provider to another then this poses potentially ego-damaging situations for the buyers. The provider of service should help the buyer to communicate effectively with their organisation to set expectations. If they subsequently beat those expectations then the reputation of both ascend. But to say nothing and have early start up glitches can cause scars that take a long time to heal. I have seen contracts have very rough times as the two parties blame each other for service or product failures. The emotions of both sides become inflamed and they rush to defend their respective positions. On many occasions this is the last business you will do with this customer even if you solve the problems and get the contract back on track.

The buyer's emotions will be particularly sensitive in this phase as they seek to show to their organisation that they have managed the right process, which resulted in the right provider having been chosen. If they have passed on your expectation management messages to their own organisation and you react promptly to resolve issues as they arise then even a less than perfect product or service will not damage the relationship. However, over promising and inattentive issue management will leave scars that may take a long time to heal. And of course infectious history means that scars are infectious!

PROBLEM HANDLING AND RESOLUTION

It is relatively easy to run an organisation when everything is running smoothly, but the sign of a highly effective organisation is how it deals with events when they do not run smoothly due to internal errors or external influences.

One of the most sensitive times in your relationship with your customers is when they have a problem. There is a wealth of evidence that shows that how you deal with product and service problems has a profound effect on the attitude of the consumer to the organisation. Prompt effective and communicative resolution of problems raises the level of trust and respect an organisation is held in rather than lowers it. It is not difficult to imagine our own feelings when we have a service or product problem. Firstly we want recognition of the problem and then actions to resolve the issue. Above all we want to be informed about progress.

I spoke with a machine tool retailer at a trade fair and he was very annoyed with one of his ex-suppliers. 'It was not that the drill broke repeatedly,' he said.' But when I asked for an explanation I was virtually ignored. Nobody gave me any ideas why. Perhaps it was being used in the wrong way. I do not know.' He no longer deals with that supplier and his feelings of being ignored and rejected came across to me strongly. If I were dealing with the organisation he was complaining about it would have given me cause for concern even if my own personal experience had not given me any evidence of this type of behaviour.

The way problems are dealt with profoundly affects your impressions of an organisation. For example an organisation that exhibited at a fair in Sweden at the Stockholm exhibition centre. When they made the initial arrangements to exhibit it was relatively easy to finalise all the necessary decisions such as stand type and associated services. They were dealt with quite professionally with lots of good information and web-based tools to order services and confirm exhibitor information. The event ran well until the day they started to close down the stand and pack up ready to go home. The exhibition logistics group could not find the specialised packing material that they had removed from the stand for safe storage on the opening day. Repeated enquiries failed to turn up the material for three days. The equipment that had been exhibited was extremely difficult to move without these specialised packing boxes. When they were eventually found, they were on the way to Germany having been sent in error instead of a heavy pipe-bending machine. Error followed error with the material being shipped back from Germany only to be incorrectly sent back yet again by the exhibition centre's logistics group in a set of bizarre moves and failures to read and act on written instructions. These events would have been more at home in an episode of *Fawlty Towers* – hardly the behaviour you would expect from a modern conference centre. Despite repeated phone calls, the organisers only started to take the problem seriously as invoices for transport costs began to land on their desks. They made an offer to waive the charges for a few minor services such as logistics. But what told me most about the organisation was when the project manager for the exhibition rang to confirm that they would resolve the problem, he said, 'Our exhibition logistics manager will ring you today with a status report. He is now taking this seriously. If you do not get a satisfactory answer please come back to me.' What did this conversation tell us:

- You are not important enough for me to follow this personally.
- We have not taken the issue seriously until now.
- The project manager does not trust his logistics manager to deal effectively with the problem and we may not be satisfied with the way he resolves the problem.

Our reaction to the organisation was one of contempt. Firstly to make a series of very silly errors and then for the project manager to give up ownership of the problem to someone who, it appears, he did not trust. Perhaps it was an attempt on his behalf to ensure the logistics manager took ownership of the problem.

He did not give a 'whatever it takes' commitment to solve the problem or offer personally to see the problem to a successful resolution. The reputation of this organisation has slid from efficient to incompetent. Based on this performance they appear to lack the professionalism to deal with customer issues effectively. The anger this sort of ineffective problem management arouses drives a desire to make sure as many people know about it as possible. Every time I visited the company's offices they were telling someone else what a mess the exhibition centre had made. Such is the stuff of infectious history.

They say 'hell has no fury like a woman scorned' but a customer who believes themselves to be badly treated comes very close. In the end many weeks later they agreed to waive a substantial part of the fees for the exhibition stand in what was a fair settlement for the direct costs their errors had produced. But by then the damage had been done as negative emotions had been passed from one aggrieved stakeholder to many other potential stakeholders.

The real issue is not that you should not make mistakes. To err is to be human. But you must have the training and processes to identify errors quickly and then to manage them to a resolution. The prime objective is to ensure that the stakeholder who is the subject of the error goes away with a positive impression of the company. If you do not achieve this, at least as many other people as you have fingers on your hands will know about the problem in graphic detail and hence the infection continues. Not managing problems effectively is either due to arrogance or ignorance. Arrogance as in, 'one small problem does not matter, what can the customer do to us, sue us?' Ignorance of the potential knock on effects, 'We all make mistakes – nobody is perfect. We can't please everybody. They will forget about it in a few days.'

To have repeated bad assessments of your performance being passed from customer to potential customer and even to be sued is definitely something they should issue a government health warning against. To ignore the cumulative effects of poor performance on reputation and then on your future financial performance is almost certainly a career-limiting defect.

BUSINESS PRESENTATIONS AND CONFERENCES

One of the ways buyers gain impressions about your organisation is through presentations from your staff, for example at conferences. As we have seen from the research findings personal experience has great potency. Presentations are a highly ranked source of information about service or product providers. They provide a chance to gather information about the organisation and to measure a key member of their staff. Organisations that take these forums seriously and ensure that their representatives give competent performances reap a positive harvest that is near impossible to quantify but is for sure a handsome return on their investment. Events you run yourselves can do immeasurable damage if they are badly managed or have ineffective speakers.

I was invited to speak at an Ericsson conference in Madrid. The pre-event information was patchy and the briefing I received on arrival was not comprehensive. It continued in the same vein with minor microphone glitches and organisational uncertainties. The Ericsson keynote speaker was excellent. Despite being Swedish born and resident, he presented in fluent Spanish. My overriding impression was of a disorganised organisation with some good people in it. I suspect Ericsson's customers and partners who were present shared this impression. On balance this was a public minus point for the company's reputation that could have been avoided. In mitigation, Ericsson was going through a tough financial period and was in the process of reducing staff – but it is particularly important at times like this not to let your public face show any signs of the turmoil inside.

Equally concerning was the response to a question from the audience by a panel of industry executives drawn from IBM Global Services, Indra, PriceWaterhouseCoopers and Accenture. The question picked up a statement I had made during my presentation. My contention was that it was much more difficult for service companies to differentiate individual services in their portfolios from those of their competition. I felt that this differentiation was far easier at the organisation level. An audience member picked this statement up and asked the panel how they differentiated themselves. None of the panel was able to give a convincing explanation of their corporate values. Their halting verbal responses were matched by insecure body language. I am sure this was an omission of the individuals not of the companies themselves but again the group scored less than a home run.

Some companies pay very great attention to the impact their events have on their audiences. IBM have employed outside research organisations to survey attendees of their seminars and conferences to measure post-event attitude change. This allows them to tune the messages and content to maximise the positive development of their reputation. In general knowing what impact you are having through research is better than simply assuming you know. Perhaps it is wiser to spend less on such events but to spend it more selectively after conducting some form of research to measure the effects.

You need also to consider carefully lower profile events but maybe highly critical presentations during the whole spectrum of contact points. During the sales process we need to be sure that a well-presented case meets the expectations of the audience and not just your own internal vision. For example an upbeat selling presentation to a technical audience might not be appropriate and vice versa. A theatrical style presentation for a very straight and strictly professional audience can equally fail to be effective. The presentation style and content needs to be appropriate. You need to be sure to whom you are presenting and what they expect of you. A professional presenter will ask many questions about the audience before composing their presentation to ensure they hit the mark.

Another vital influence point is during educational situations, be they external or internal. You may well be influencing your future employees or existing employees in the early stages in their careers. Failing to impress and be relevant does great damage, which may lay dormant and unseen to you but becomes a negative element of infectious history.

CUSTOMER-FACING STAFF

The behaviour of your key sales and customer-facing staff is a huge influence on your corporate reputation. Your sales team is the highly visible expression of the corporation's business ambitions. Whether your go-to-market model is to sell directly to end-users, or indirectly to resellers or partners, they hold the keys to a large part of how your organisation is perceived. Some sales organisations have a culture that considers potential and existing customers to be adversaries over whom they must prevail. This gives a propensity for them to use a derogatory and condescending approach to their ultimate source of sustenance, in their terminology 'the punters'. This disrespectful viewpoint is in effect biting the hand that feeds you! Conversely organisations that try to partner with customers and to understand their unique and industry-related issues generally build the most durable long-term relationships and the most valued reputations. The attitudes and behaviour of your customer-facing staff reflects the health of your organisation.

Your sales team needs to be well trained and motivated. Everyday they meet customers and exude unspoken signals about their attitudes towards your organisation. They may also be more outspoken in their criticism faced with customer issues to resolve. The insecure and unprofessional salesman can often lapse into, 'what have those idiots in accounts done this time?' Only by training, effective management and motivation can you give them the confidence to work through issues and not resort to the easy way out. If they have a tendency to take this type of short cut the research may well reveal symptoms of this.

Some years ago EDS felt it had a problem of reputation with its customers. It undertook extensive research to understand their feelings. The findings showed that EDS people were considered arrogant and that service problems were not resolved until they became sufficiently grave to attract the attention of senior managers. EDS acted on the finding and attempted to change their internal culture of suppressing rather than revealing issues. They also started to present themselves publicly in a more self-deprecating light. They developed a series of television advertisements, which depicted themselves as cat wranglers, and builders of aeroplanes while they were flying. The cowboys herding cats advertisement was first shown during the American Super Bowl and attracted a highly positive response. The voiceover explained how tough these cats were to handle while macho cowboys were seen herding them across the prairies. The advertisements were publicly explained as attempting to show they had a core competence to manage complex situations. But in reality it was designed to give themselves a more cuddly image and distance themselves from the Ross Perrot heritage.

But nice adverts alone will not change anything for long unless the people at the sharp end also change their behaviour to reflect the public image of the organisation.

Every day customer interaction affects your reputation. By regularly surveying customers and mapping the points at which a customer touches your organisation and how these onstage touch points are supported by backstage actions and processes helps you to understand the customer experience. Once the touch points are mapped you can work to ensure all the actors both onstage and back stage see themselves from the customers perspective and are motivated to try to ensure the best possible customer experience subject of course to the limits of the resources available.

The telephone organisation that has a call centre you can never get through to without a 20 minute wait, and the insurance organisation that advertises a Saturday emergency call service which is never actually available – leave you with a bitter taste in your mouth that shoots one arrow in their corporate reputation. I suspect you would only want to do business with these sorts of organisations if the price is very low to compensate you for your wasted time.

Another area of concern for your reputation is not only the effects of your staff on customers and prospects but also their effect on the media. In recent years there has been a lot of attention paid to creating a better workplace. Many organisations are trying to find better ways to work and support their staff. Trying to reduce stress and eliminate behaviour such as bullying and harassment, sexual or otherwise, have received high profile media coverage. According to the Industrial Society, 270,000 employees in the UK take days off due to stress. Each sick day cost an estimated £487 for each employee and £12 billion to the UK economy.

High profile sexual harassment or bullying cases do not help your reputation. Staff that are stressed and feeling bullied are much less likely to provide excellent customer care and attention. If you believe your problems lie in this direction perhaps reading this book will not give you the returns you hoped for. I suggest you find something on best practice in personnel management. Any efforts you make to improve your reputation are unlikely to succeed if your staff are not willing and motivated players in the game.

MEDIA COVERAGE

The attention of the media also has a profound impact on reputation. The public relations sector has many excellent practitioners who guide organisations through the perils of media relations. But their efforts need to be complimented by informed and effective communicators within your organisation. I have seen solid PR opportunities lost when senior executives present, to the media, myopic visions in which their organisations are placed at the centre of the world. Their understandable pride in their organisation can be inappropriately expressed. Another potential issue is sometimes they see the well-informed young journalist in front of them as a junior employee to be lectured rather than a person who has the power to significantly influence the corporation's future. The 'alpha' qualities that are demanded to fight your way to the top of, or build, an organisation do not necessarily come with the empathy to listen to and show careful respect for apparently more junior people. It is important never to forget that whatever they do the world is watching.

Ryanair in 2002 was ordered to pay damages of 67,500 euros to a passenger after a judge found the airline had reneged on a promise to give her free flights for life. Jane O'Keeffe had been given the free flights after becoming the airline's one-millionth passenger in 1988. But she sued Ryanair for damages after she claimed the organisation was refusing to honour the prize. Mr Justice Peter Kelly found that the airline had breached its contract with Ms O'Keeffe when it started to restrict the offer in 1997. Ryanair had argued that there was no legal contract between the organisation and Ms O'Keeffe, and that the offer was a gift. Ms O'Keeffe had won the prize in a blaze of publicity, with widespread media coverage. She had used the offer up until 1997 without any problems, despite the lack of a written contract. The judge said her use of free travel was 'modest'. 'During most years she took three or four flights and certainly never exceeded five,' he said. But in 1997 she started to have problems, which came to a head when she attempted to book a flight from Dublin to Glasgow. She complained to the airline, but the judge said her treatment by Ryanair over the incident had been 'unpleasant and shabby'. He also said Ryanair's chief executive had been 'hostile and aggressive' in his dealings with her.

It is difficult to see this any other way than as corporate arrogance: to award a benefit in a fanfare of publicity and then take it away. To add insult to injury and then to allow them to sue you and win in the full sight of the media is, to say the least, careless. The impact on Ryanair's fast growing low cost airline business is not likely to be immediately financially significant but many months later the media was still reporting Ryanair's quarterly results with the reminder of the court ruling and the comment that the public image of the organisation and Ryanair Chief Executive Michael O'Leary had been tarnished. The BBC covered the annual report of the Air Transport Users Council for the year ended April 2002 with the headline.

'Ryanair rejects "poor service" report. Cheap, but not necessarily cheerful Ryanair has hit back at a report which shows passengers thought its standards were some of the worst in the world.'

In fact it showed Ryanair were third in the list of complaints behind British Airways and Air France. The media love to attack what they see as hypocrisy. Claim you are the consumer's champion and then make a mistake like Ryanair and they pounce on you with great delight.

You choose Ryanair for price not service but how many people selected another provider rather than Ryanair around the time of the media coverage is impossible to measure. The low cost airline sector is becoming increasingly competitive and failure to protect reputations may well bring negative impacts in the future.

Another example of the candid camera effect is the case of Martha Stewart. The US-based media and retail company Martha Stewart Living Omnimedia reported a 42 per cent fall in net profits for the July to September 2002 quarter. The company blamed rising costs and warned of further weakness during the rest of this year. The reality is that the CEO and founder of the company had been the subject of insider trading allegations.

The first stakeholders to desert the company were its investors. They sold Martha Stewart stock when the news first appeared in the media. The stock price dropped by half in six months. Investors continued to dump the stock after the latest financial news. They feared that the poor performance was evidence of the firm's customers being unhappy to do business with the company.

The scandal related to Martha Stewart's sale of shares in ImClone Systems, a pharmaceutical company, one day before US regulators ruled unfavourably on the company's cancer drug. Lawyers at the Securities and Exchange Commission had warned Ms Stewart they were prepared to pursue civil securities fraud charges against her.

INDUSTRY WATCHERS

Industry analysts have gained credibility over the years as sources of advice about which companies to invite to bid, how to manage bids and even what the contracts should look like. Their influence is significant and organisations such as IDC, Forrester, Ovum, and Gartner lead the pack. Gartner cut its teeth as the adviser to the chief information officer and has retained a strong base of influence in the IT end user sector. They report on and rank suppliers. Having a positive reputation with people like Gartner is obviously desirable. Unless you are a substantial player in a market or you are of particular niche interest then it is sometimes difficult to attract the attention of the industry analysts relevant to your business. However with modest investments and a little subtlety you can leverage positive messages from these sources and positively impact your reputation.

Undoubtedly in your mapping of influencers of reputation the Industry analysts need to be carefully researched to understand their influence. Many investment analysts turn to the industry analysts for organisation and market-specific information and views. The potential for the analyst to influence your reputation will depend greatly on the sector and type of business you are operating in but it is never safe to assume they have little impact at all.

In summary

These are some of the scenarios and actors in our corporate drama, and some of the moments when your reputation can be significantly affected. Perhaps it should be said that I am not suggesting that you can forget cash flow, product differentiation, market positioning, brand awareness and the wealth of other factors that make up the corporate health guide. However, even if you have all the above right but your reputation is not in line with your corporate ambitions, it can cause you to become extinct or to limp along seriously underperforming against your potential. In the hectic business world it is difficult to avoid being swept along by the crowd of colleagues marching to the sounds of your corporate drums. But finding out whether your other stakeholders are marching with you or are simply watching you fade into the distance is not just *nice to know* it is *essential* to know.

4 360° Mapping of Stakeholder Influence

Well we know how we may have been awarded our reputation. Now we need to identify the individual people concerned and how they interact with each other. Once we know who they are we can conduct research to find out what they feel about our organisation and how these feelings and opinions are passed on to other stakeholders. A key part in the process is to understand and map the ways each stakeholder group interacts with other stakeholders. In this chapter we will look at the first steps in a process of measuring and managing your reputation. We will discuss the importance of fact-based research and the necessity to survey a wide spectrum of stakeholders to understand their feelings. From our mapping we will find that many and diverse groups of stakeholders have a material impact on forming our reputation. It is not only our customers whose opinions we need to be aware of but also the other groups and individuals who are influencing them.

So why do we need to do research? Why cannot selected managers just talk to our stakeholders to understand what they feel about us without all this expense and effort?

Fact-based marketing as a core principle

Yes you could just talk to stakeholders, but what would you end up with? The stakeholders will not have given anything close to frank and honest answers. Frankness and honesty to people we know, or have regular dealings with, is very rare. Each of the managers will probably have their own agendas to fulfil and will bend the already unreliable responses to their particular persuasion. Nobody will trust each other's analysis so probably no concrete actions will result from the findings. The activity can be consigned to the opinions about opinions pigeonhole.

The key quality of a *fact-based* approach is to try not to act on hunches and assumptions but rather on independently obtained data. However this does not work in all marketing situations. We should be aware of the limitations of research when you are attempting to develop for instance new approaches or new products. If a researcher had asked very early man what they wanted most it may have been:

- A way to move food stores more quickly than on sleds. To protect them from the hairy mammoth and the attention of other tribes.
- A way to travel faster every day with all the things we need to live. So we can occupy territory we win from other tribes more quickly.

They would not have asked for the wheel. But if they were to attach wheels to their sleds they would have achieved their objectives. Yet more difficult still is when we are not able even to articulate the need. We only know we want it when we see it. Did you know you wanted a skateboard before you saw one?

Research within a fact-based marketing approach works best when it is analysing and measuring current preferences, feelings or responses to perhaps corporate, product or service attributes. Anecdotal methods of measurement for reputation research provide too sparse and too modified information on which to act. The only way we are likely to produce actionable data is via a formal, fact based 360° research programme.

Taking a 360° view of your reputation

To move the process on we know need specifically to identify who our stakeholders actually are and how they interact. One of the most useful exercises is to map out your stakeholders and to try to understand how they influence your corporate reputation. Taking a global view of all your key stakeholders will provide a more complete view of the dynamics that have created your reputation. Many of the stakeholders will influence each other. The media and analysts provide a background of comments that affect potential employees, customers, potential customers, the investment community and your staff. Equally, peer-to-peer comments of buyers within existing and potential customers will influence your ability to appear on the bid lists for new opportunities. Your partners influence each other and customers and so on.

We need to build a complete picture of the organisations and the individuals within these organisations that form your reputation. You will have to assume the influences and impacts they have on each other based on your current knowledge and generic research. You may feel you need to conduct additional research to understand how these stakeholders impact each other, particularly in critical processes such as buying or the influence of the industry analysts on your customers. Do not be put off by what appears to be the prospect of a large bill for research. The exploration of stakeholders' influence over each other can be realised with very modest investment via a few telephone interviews and conversations. Once you have a map of whom, you believe influences whom and how, you can develop a programme of research to understand your reputation with these groups and individuals.

CUSTOMER AND PROSPECTS

We need to identify, individually, the key people within your customers and prospects who influence your business opportunities. To achieve this we need to fully understand the buying process within your customer and prospects. How do they arrive at bidder shortlists? Who are the key individuals who influence or decide? What are the processes they use to arrive at the final decision?

If you believe you know this information already it is still advisable to insert a section on this subject in your customer research to confirm or refine your knowledge. The questions are completed only if the person being interviewed plays a role in the buying process. If you are not very sure about how it works in your prospects then a small research project will help you to identify the critical people and the process steps. If you do not know this information already you will find it enlightening and a sound investment. If you choose the alternative to wait and research this aspect only during the general customer research then you will need to build your target list of influencers and decision makers based on best guesses.

If you have a well-managed Customer Relationship Management system or something similar then you will be able to generate the required names relatively easily. If not, then you will probably have to approach the sales team to gather the necessary data. Here you could meet your first stumbling block. Sales teams are notoriously protective of their customers and prospects. In many organisations this vital data, which has cost the organisation a great deal of effort and money to build, rests at very worst in the heads of the sales team or in a paper-based system. Usually the list is not wide enough and is probably not up to date. Sales teams normally resist giving up the names of contacts without a very full explanation as to the intentions for the use of the list. They may fight hard not to give their agreement. This is, perhaps, a case of the tail wagging the dog. But in many cases the sales teams have this power to resist. Their motivation is clear. Publicly they will probably say they want to ensure correct and sensitive account management is maintained, they do not want to see their customers disturbed by inappropriate activity. Here is, of course, fallacy number one: the customer belongs to the whole organisation not to the sales team alone. More likely their real motivation is to retain the power of knowledge and negotiation. Many sales teams move their organisations by using 'the customer says they want' as their primary lever, and they do not like to give up any of that leverage easily. They also like to keep the mystique that they alone know how to deal with customers and prospects. But there is more than a grain of truth in all of this. Account management integrity and ensuring activity with prospective customers is appropriate and professional and is vital. But many a sales team reacts with duplicity and obstruction when you legitimately request assistance from them to collect this highly valuable asset of the organisation. If you meet very stiff resistance then perhaps it would be wise to delay this activity until you have the buy-in of the executive team for a reputation, management research project.

If you understand the buying process fully then you have gone a long way to understanding who are some of the most critical recipients of your reputation. I have met some sales teams that follow the bid process and have no real understanding of the process being followed, who are the critical players in the process and what they may feel about the organisation, while other sales teams have been past masters at understanding and even manipulating this process. An ex-colleague, Dan Pegg, seemed to spend more of his time analysing and understanding the internal power battles and relationships in his customers than he ever did 'selling'. His results were always outstanding. This was not a hurried activity carried out only at the time of responding to a bid but an ongoing process of discovery. He invited his internal sponsors within the customers periodically to discuss with his sales team how they could more effectively manage the customer or prospect. He encouraged the sponsor to speculate and identify the feelings and attitudes of his colleagues towards his organisation and how those attitudes could be made more positive. He then laid out an ongoing strategy to manage the perception of the organisation in thoughtful account planning and review sessions.

This kind of process is only possible where the value of business generated justifies the investment but it pays enormous dividends. It provides a customer-by-customer mapping of decision makers and influencers. Within this map, individual strategies are formed for each key decision maker and influencer. However when the value of each individual customer does not support this type of approach then research to build the typical model of the process and its key actors is a more cost-effective solution. Here, using an outside organisation to conduct the research for you often produces a more truthful and balanced picture while internally produced research may well fall into the 'opinions about opinions' category. A modest project over a few days can yield interesting results.

With potential customers we could follow the same process either by a case-by-case study of the individual organisation or a generic survey to identify the most usual processes and actors.

THE MEDIA

You must be able to identify the media that influences the key actors within your customers and potential customers, if you are to target the main influencers of your corporate reputation. Without this information identifying the media that has the most influence on your reputation will be guesswork. Obviously you will be primarily concerned with the influencers of your more immediate business opportunities, but you should also understand which media reaches and is valued by your employees, potential employees, investors and partners.

If you are a local player and not a large organisation you will probably not have to worry about the national media. It is of no use to research your reputation with people who have not heard of you; it is more useful to hear what your local media think about you and to identify all the coverage you have received in the last year to see what it is saying about you and who is saying it.

You may not have all the necessary data to identify all the right media so a little guesswork will suffice. In the later research you can introduce questions about which media influences each stakeholder group to extend your knowledge. You may well decide to leave research into media attitudes until a little later in the project and by then the results from customers and staff will be known so selecting the media influencers to survey will have some data to guide you.

INDUSTRY ANALYSTS

They are not so numerous that you cannot quite quickly identify the companies and individuals who need to be researched. Identify the companies and then ask them to tell you who are their industry specialists for your sectors.

Hopefully you will start this process before they have taken a less than positive stance towards your organisation. In my experience once they have a negative opinion about your organisation it takes a great deal of effort to improve it. Analysts do not seem to like to change their minds too quickly unless they appear to be fickle or unsure of themselves. If you need help to identify the industry analysts that matter to you, a few specialist firms exist that can help you. But at a minimum, if you can spare an appropriate person to spend part of their time on this activity they can identify and subsequently lead the process of managing analysts, relationships without great difficulty.

FINANCIAL ANALYSTS

These will also be relatively easy to identify as organisations and individuals, and they probably are asking you for information already. It perhaps can wait until later in the plan to investigate this area unless you have some pressing reason to do so right now. If you are concerned about your share price or contemplating a stock market flotation then obviously you will have this group higher up the priority list. They probably do not overly influence your new business opportunities unless of course they are about to publicly down rate you from a hold to a sell recommendation that might have some reputation impact.

PARTNERS

You know your partners and you are probably communicating with them on a regular basis so identifying them as companies and individuals should be trivial. Partners can seriously affect your reputation. If your brother says you are not to be trusted this will have a greater impact than if your worst enemy expresses the same view – the closeness of partners gives them both knowledge and believability. But because of the way we include partners into our organisations it is often assumed that they share our views and ambitions, which in fact may not be the case. We also can tend to ignore the need to communicate effectively with long-term partners believing they know us too well.

Partners who may be both customers and part of the service or product delivery chain are significant stakeholders. Their attitudes and behaviour can substantially impact your reputation. Many organisations that have substantial partner networks have extensive programmes to ensure they meet the standards of the organisation in their commercialisation of their products and services. Partners live in the twilight zone of not being internal to the organisation but also not being external. They often know many people within your organisation and may have dealt with the organisation for a number of years. Managing partner relationships requires delicacy and consistency.

Partner management is a delicate specialisation that requires empathy and discipline in equal measures. Often you need to remind your organisation that a partner is not part of your organisation and the commercial realities must be respected. Partners need to be sold too and communicated with as effectively, if not more so, as your best customers.

The risk with partners is they find internal routes to information, support, resources and influence that produce high-unseen costs. Long-term partners can fall into the 'familiarity breeds contempt' trap from either side. Keeping them well informed about your developments and understanding theirs is critical. Asking them regularly how they feel about the organisation may produce interesting results. Hewlett Packard wanted to understand how to communicate effectively with their partners. They took a small group of them off site for a couple of days to discuss the issue. What they found startled them. The partners complained of waves of documents and information flowing over them, most of which they did not read. The flow was neither managed nor controlled. Often critical information came late but in beautifully formatted documents. One respondent commented that it was better to receive 'a timely handwritten fax rather than a printed document that is late!' The partners complained that most of the major suppliers they dealt with were the same. Hewlett Packard changed the way they communicated based on this research. With partners you may be 'married' but you have to ask yourself the question 'are you still lovers?'

EMPLOYEES

Your employees are key influencers and stakeholders of corporate reputation. We need to map them into our stakeholder influence matrix. Customer-facing and sales staff probably have the most direct influence on corporate reputation, while the rest of the organisation makes a less direct contribution but is equally concerned with the organisation's reputation. We all would prefer to work for an organisation that we feel is well thought of and respected. It feels much better to go to the pub when you know people have heard of whom you work for and have some positive reaction towards your organisation. This may rely more on the above the water brand portion but people with knowledge of your industry will also be affected by your reputation. Ryanair employees must have felt a little apprehensive about their social engagement after the news of the court case hit the headlines.

In balancing your research activities you may wish to bias your research in terms of sample size towards those staff who actually are customer-facing. This may be by using more face-to-face interviews with them rather than say web-based survey tools. Certainly, you cannot rely only on web or email surveying of your staff. You need some good conversations with your researchers to understand fully what they feel and what they understand about your organisation.

This data will be vital to fully understand how your staff reconcile corporate organisational objectives and the customer's feelings and requirements. Staff must know how to please their customers and why it matters to them. They should understand and be able to explain your organisational objectives. Your corporate messaging needs to be able to help them to achieve this objective. These messages should be both aspirational and believable. This is where we are trying to go. So understanding the current status of our staff's views and feelings is a critical element in the 360° puzzle.

A friend of mine was offered a position with Computer Associates. Some of his friends advised him strongly against taking the job as Computer Associates, they had heard, had a reputation for being hard-nosed and tough to work for. He did in fact take the job and appears to be happy. But how many other people have this company and countless others lost because the applicants decided instead to take a friend's advice?

How you appear as an employer will influence your ability to attract talent. If you need to recruit staff in a competitive market then you might want to add potential employees to your survey. This can be tough to accomplish unless you have a well-defined target audience such as university graduates. One alternative is to interview recently hired staff and perhaps some of the organisations you have used to obtain those staff such as employment and recruitment agencies.

Building an influence map of stakeholders

Once you have a list of stakeholder groups and the individuals within these groups you can start to prioritise them depending on their impact on your reputation and your business objectives. Deciding how to prioritise the different stakeholders and allot an importance and urgency to them is the next step.

If you are recruiting staff and planning to float on the stock exchange in the near future then you may well place a high priority on investment analysts and industry analysts. If you are facing tough competition in a core market then your focus may well be customers and prospects. If you have an indirect go-to-market model then your partners and customers will be high priorities. But you still need to cover all the stakeholder groups. This prioritisation is merely deciding where you think you need to put either more effort or early efforts but not *everything*. There is no way you can miss out a group and have the full picture. This will leave you perhaps making the wrong decisions when you decide how to respond to the research.

The list of companies and individuals who affect your reputation

The lists you build will be used to select the people to be interviewed. They will contain organisations and individuals who have most impact on your reputation and are most influenced by it. But do not draw the net too tightly within your customers and your prospects. Ensure you include people within these groups who are not necessarily the key decision makers or high-level influencers. Remember that in any social structure the rumour and reputation machine includes users of the service and other people who are involved with you regularly.

When you finally start the process of interviewing, the research team will select from this list. They will select a representative sample, as far as they are able, without being influenced by your organisation's preferences. The sales team will put forward names of people they hope will be positive to them firstly and your organisation secondly. The service delivery team will likewise select friendly voices. You will find a shortage of candidates from customers who have had issues with you and a weighting towards those who will provide glowing references. A skilled research team will recognise this bias and extend themselves out of the list to round out the research with a balanced sample as far as this is possible. They will use one or more contacts within the organisation to point them to additional people who might be useful to interview. All research is flawed, to some degree, by bias in the sample and the effects of simply asking the questions on the subjects interviewed. But, like democracy, it may be a lousy system but there is no other viable alternative.

Try very hard to ensure that the survey is based on a list that is genuinely representative of all likely shades of opinions. If conversely, you just want to follow your prejudices and fix the results to say what you want them to say then I believe you will come to regret that decision. The story of the king and his new suit of clothes springs to mind.

When you are this far down the process I recommend you bring in external help if you have not done so already. An external consultant, if you have chosen correctly, comes with their preconceptions about your organisation and industry tightly under control. They can give you a sanity check on the work you have done so far to understand who are your key stakeholders and what the matrix of influence between them may be. If you intend to take this process to the point of conducting research into your corporate reputation within key stakeholder groups, a consultant can help to ensure any survey is as objective as possible and consistent.

The consultants can share their experience of the relative influence of groups like the media and the industry analysts. They can explore with you the actors in the bidding process and help to place importance on who is the most critical to research and influence. They can also be vital to help you sell the concepts of reputation management in the next vital step.

5 Building Executive Commitment to Measure your Reputation and the Key Role of Communications

An essential next step in the process is to win executive commitment. One effective approach is to gather a small group of key executives responsible for all of the key corporate functions together for a workshop. If you are serious in your quest to research and manage your reputation then having the buy-in and understanding of your executive team is vital. In many cases the research findings will demand significant changes to internal behaviour, processes and attitudes. These types of changes demand commitment from senior management. They need to 'walk the talk' or the desired changes will not be achieved. Hopefully you are either a member of the executive team or you have identified a sponsor to guide you through this vital step.

Executive workshop

The objective of this meeting is to raise the issue of your reputation, and its potential impacts, to start the process of buy-in from the key management team and to gain commitment to spending the money necessary for a meaningful research project.

Having an outside moderator and presenter who can talk convincingly from personal experience will greatly assist in getting the executive team onside. They can also give some ballpark figures for the likely costs of undertaking an effective research programme.

A TYPICAL AGENDA

The workshop might start with a presentation of the available evidence showing how reputation influences corporate results. This is the key point. If you are not convincing at this stage then the game may well be over. It is dangerous to focus too much on the sudden death scenarios for corporate reputation failure. In practice no research would have helped Andersen or Living Omnimedia to avoid their problems. I suggest you focus on the chronic illness implications, explaining that every day of every year we are being affected and we do not know how and what this means to us. Human nature is inclined to ignore the threat of sudden death; we are also disposed to assume that we have good reputations even if we admit they may not be spotless. Often we avoid the truth in case we do not like what we hear. Gaining a true understanding of the power of reputation is not an easy task.

The conditioning of business life is to think in terms of the mantras – often repeated but not always understood:

- market positioning
- technology leadership
- price performance
- brand recognition
- return on investment
- customer focused
- feature, benefit, advantage.

In the face of this conditioning senior executives may take some time to admit that it is your reputation, which of course is the perception of your ability to respond to the core issues behind the mantras, that embodies the essence of the organisation. It is your reputation that attracts or rejects the people who decide your future. It is your reputation that allows your stakeholders to place you in your appropriate position in the corporate solar system. After all we do not decide where we will be positioned but it is our stakeholders who decide our fate. We can aspire but they decide.

You need to have solid anecdotal evidence which points to reputational issues within your own organisation. The key idea to impart is the ambition to achieve an appropriate reputation for your organisational ambitions. Try to steer away from thoughts of good or bad reputations, as this is frankly not useful.

If you have won the day on the first key point now we can set the stage for the right approach. A presentation of some of the key attributes of fact-based marketing can help to introduce the concept of data's ascendancy over assumption. It is important to bear in mind the old adage that 'Assumption makes an ass out of you and me', it is wise not to 'ASS U ME'. Having data to back up your claims will be a far more powerful base from which to persuade your organisation to make any necessary changes.

The 360° mapping of stakeholders can be presented next to show activity undertaken to date, and the group can then be invited to discuss how they believe these individuals and groups interact with each other. They should avoid creating assumptions about what your reputation is today with key stakeholders. The meeting needs to be directed to realise that without objective analysis you do not know what your reputation really is. The object of the workshop is to *introduce* the concepts, *establish* the disciplines, *and explain* the relevancy and to *involve* a key group of managers in contributing to the process.

The meeting needs to focus on who and what influences whom and how significant is that interaction assumed to be. One of the ways to achieve this is to consider an external case study of one of your organisation's current suppliers and to discuss how they have given you their reputation. This reputation may vary between each individual in the room but it will be much easier to have an objective view of how that perception of their reputation was arrived at using a third party as the subject. When this process is concluded your own influence mapping could be tackled. But the key objective of the workshop is for the executive team to accept the influence of reputation on the organisation's future. Mapping who influences who and deciding which groups and who to interview first is a secondary objective.

MANAGING DEPARTMENTAL AGENDAS

Departmental agendas may well rise to the surface during the workshop.

- The marketing director, if he or she is leading this activity, may push for an in depth research project. They could see this as an opportunity to gain budget and achieve some long held objectives. These objectives, however honourable, need to be kept in check. We want *to know enough but not everything* and it would be wrong to discredit the objective by over-ambitious and costly projects. If marketing is not running the process it will almost certainly feel threatened. It may feel that its understanding of the organisation's customers and your external image is in question, which of course may well be true.
- The sales director may have severe reservations about the process. They may be afraid it will disturb their customers, expose some of the sales teams failings and reveal that they do not understand their customers as well as they should.
- Your service delivery team can feel threatened by both the prospect of changes to existing processes and to their self-respect about their ability to deliver service.
- The human relations team may fear the staff disruption and additional workload generated by any attitude change programme motivated by the research results.
- The financial director could ask if this is really necessary when the results are looking as good as they are right now. Or even more alarmingly we cannot afford this sort of diversion and cost with results as bad as they are right now!

If you meet these types of objections then you need to press on and carry out this research with vigour and resolution. If your senior management team is not really interested or frightened to find out what your key stakeholders think about your organisation, then they are not listening attentively to them. In my experience the organisations that resist this approach the most and are least concerned with understanding their reputation are usually the organisations that could benefit most from it. Organisations with strong culture and long traditions, run by dominant management and that are successful in their sectors could be considered suitable cases for treatment. Perhaps this may have been the case with Marks & Spencer prior to their management changes and the arrival of Luc Vandevelde.

If you enthusiastically accept and implement the concepts of reputation management you may well discover some significant findings that will demand changes, which will result in improvements to your reputation and which will positively impact your financial future.

This critical meeting is targeted to achieve a number of objectives.

- An *understanding* of the influence corporate reputation has over your financial success.
- An *appreciation* of the disciplines of fact-based marketing.
- *Who* are your organisation's key stakeholders?
- *How* they are likely to influence each other.
- *Which* corporate processes also influence reputation most?
- A *commitment* to develop a plan to find the facts via a research project and an approximate budget.

If you can achieve these objectives they are significant steps forward. The project should now be well and truly launched. You should have established the three key elements for a successful project: funding, authority and need.

Where should we find the resources to carry out the research – internally or externally?

The next step is to decide how you will carry out the research. The project will involve extensive interviewing of stakeholders. This is a resource-heavy activity and hence you might not plan to do it all in one shot. It can be carried out via a programme that extends over a number of months to spread the cost and workload. You can leave some of the stakeholder groups until last to use some of the data from the earlier groups to focus your questions. In preparing your plan you will need to decide whether it should be wholly outsourced to a qualified organisation or carried out with internal resources. To give the research projects a uniformity of approach and hence a greater relevancy it is better to select one organisation to complete all the research activities for all of the groups. This approach also introduces both an efficiency derived from repetition plus a single view of all the data that can be very powerful.

I have tried to outline some of the pros and cons of using an external resource below.

THE PLUS POINTS FOR USING AN EXTERNAL RESOURCE

- Objective analysis with no agenda to obscure the findings.
- The results may not be complimentary and hence there is a danger of the 'shoot the messenger' problem. Perhaps it's better to have an outside bearer of bad news.
- An experienced research team will have the necessary experience and skills. They are more likely to complete the work quickly and be able to advise on sample sizes.
- An experienced team will switch resource dynamically when they find the same repeated results for one group. This resource can be redirected to groups where the results are not coming as easily. This helps to ensure all stakeholder groups in the survey are covered adequately within the budgeted costs.
- Having an outside organisation design and ask the questions will probably produce more truthful answers from the interviewees.
- The necessary internal resource may well not be available for the period necessary to complete the work.

THE ARGUMENTS AGAINST USING AN EXTERNAL RESOURCE

- The costs can be high if the groups and sample sizes are large. But significant results can be achieved with budgets that are very modest.
- If you do not have a practice of using external groups for critical projects, the activity can be seen as non-core or intrusive if an external group is used to complete the work and hence may be more easily ignored.
- Developing the internal discipline to carry out this type of activity ensures that a corporate awareness of reputation management is institutionalised.

In most cases I recommend that an experienced external research organisation should be selected. The benefits of objectivity and experience in research means you will obtain a result more quickly and reliably. Ideally their work should be specified and reviewed by a senior management team. This is to ensure that the results will be accepted and hopefully drive action to improve those areas that are found to require attention. If the executive group has not been through an intensive day of executive briefing then there is some risk of the research being diverted into other objectives. You need to watch this carefully and indeed if the executive team has not already understood the objectives and accepted them then your chances of a highly successful project are diminished.

The outside research team should use their experience to ensure the research methods and questions do not allow internal agendas and bias to creep in. The senior management team must be willing to explain to the group building the questionnaire the organisation's future development plans so that this can be factored into the timing of the stakeholder groups covered and the questions asked.

The scale and complexity of the project

One of the questions you have in your mind might be: 'How long will all this research take and how many people do we need to talk to?' The answer is 'How long is a piece of string?' No I am not trying to be facetious as it depends entirely on the size and complexity of your organisation. If we assume a medium-sized organisation operating in a single country the estimates below should be reasonable.

The project to set up mapping and list building is difficult to estimate as it is dependent on the quality of the data and systems you have in house. The time to complete the major parts of the research should be within a month to six weeks in most cases. The number of people you need to interview is of course in part dependent on the numbers of people in each stakeholder group. But you need to have around 30 to 40 face-to-face or telephone interviews for the larger groups or until you consistently receive the same answers.

The sample sizes for your staff will depend on the numbers involved. If you are a very large organisation having everyone invited to contribute will not give you significantly better results if you receive answers from thousands rather than hundreds. You can use an anonymous response tool on an intranet or Web site to give everybody a chance to contribute and in this case the data assessment is not too onerous. But you must have face-to-face interviews with perhaps 30 to 40 of your staff and this demands careful reading and analysis to fully understand the messages they are giving you. Having too big a sample may well be overkill and raise the costs higher than they need to be. Remember we are seeking quality not quantity. The interviews are quite long and in depth – they need to be 40 minutes to ensure an interviewer interviewee relationship is formed and the right level of candour is achieved. The second twenty minutes will almost always be the most fruitful period of the interview. The qualities of the interviewer are critical in this type of research to ensure they develop empathy with their interviewees.

SELECTING THE RIGHT TYPE OF PEOPLE TO CARRY OUT THE RESEARCH

The questions asked and the lengths of the interviews are not as important as the attitude of the people carrying out the survey. They need to have the ability to listen carefully to the responses they are given and be able to ask secondary questions to explore and understand a response. They must be able to be intuitive about what the responses mean but not to follow agendas of their own. When you interview a potential researcher and they are prepared to respond enthusiastically about their perception of your reputation then you probably do not have the right person for the task. They need to have the attitude of, 'I do not know and my task is to find out'. Or 'I of course have an opinion. Your organisation is too well known to avoid this, but my opinions are not what counts.'

If you decide to carry out the research with your own staff this issue of objectivity really is a significant issue. You might choose to have a consultant advise and act as 'devil's advocate' at the questionnaire and stakeholder group selection stage to ensure it is objective. They can also help to do a peer review of the data and findings to ensure no agendas have crept into the results.

The role of communications in managing reputation

Having an objective and revealing research project is the first key step in a reputation management programme. But one of the key corporate qualities that will have influenced your reputation historically and will greatly influence the outcome of your project is your organisation's ability to communicate internally and externally.

Reputation is built by infectious history. We cannot change history but we can change our futures. Once you have identified the attitudes and feelings of your stakeholder the next step will be to understand the causes of those feelings and opinions you would like to modify. This will probably entail making changes of behaviour and you will need to communicate the reasons for these changes effectively. A new strap-line or three-line corporate mission statement is unlikely to do the trick. More fundamental behavioural and organisational changes may well be required.

The role of effective communications is important in any organisation at any time but when you are trying to implement change it is critical. Ensuring your key managers have the right level of skills and training to communicate effectively is vital.

THE IMPORTANCE OF A CLEAR CORPORATE STORY

Of course it is not only *how* you communicate but also *what* that matters. Your communications platform is one of the critical elements upon which your reputation is built. I am often surprised that many large organisations have somewhat disjointed stories. Their mission, strategy, beliefs, products, and so on are not linked together in a holistic way. Even if your key executives are excellent communicators taking the time to ensure they have consistent information and messages is key. Disjointed stories need to be reconsidered and a holistic, realistic and believable story built in its place. You need to express the realities and the aspirations of the organisation. It should be a key challenge to every CEO and executive group to ensure they have their story straight. Every idea, word and picture has to say something relevant. You are what people allow you to be, not what you think you are. If you do not communicate effectively you will always be less than you could have been. One of the key outputs from a reputation management plan is to ensure that all the messages to all the stakeholder groups are believable and consistent.

Your executive team has the lead role as communicators to staff, customers, analysts, partners and media. A core role of a CEO is to make decisions that are clear, understood, well timed and well communicated. Communications and media workshops are an excellent investment for your senior executives.

However getting 'A' personality types to invest time and effort in improving the way they communicate may well be a tough objective to achieve. To suggest training or a workshop is perhaps going to be seen as a criticism of their abilities in this area. If you have not been able to kick this executive training off before the findings are known then you need to include it in a wider programme of training that is motivated by the research findings. Build in a module as part of the global reputation management project and draw in the top executives as example setters. If the findings suggest some significant changes to process, behaviour or messaging then starting at the top and starting early is vital.

The executive team's ability to explain the core values of the organisation is a vital element in building and maintaining a positive reputation with stakeholders. Senior executives have gained their place in the organisation for many reasons. For them to reach a senior level they must have a well-developed ability to communicate. However this skill may be more focused on an internal audience. With effort, significant enhancements can be made to their abilities to communicate to external audiences. Performances often improve dramatically once they understand their audiences better. Effective training focuses on explaining the motivations, needs, feelings and lives of the key audiences they are meeting. Often a lack of understanding of the audience inhibits the speakers true personality being revealed and prevents empathy from developing. Helping them to relax and allow a human and believable character to emerge may well be a welcome release for the executive who will start to see a more positive feedback to their communication from the tougher external audiences.

Helping executives to understand the audiences they will be addressing can only improve their ability to be relevant and informative. The core of such training must be to show what are their potential audiences aspirations when being communicated with; how their audience feels and what it expects rather than what the speaker feels and what the speaker wants to say. The key to being an effective speaker is to have sufficient command of both your subject and the basic techniques of public speaking that you have the bandwidth during you presentation to constantly observe and feel how your audience is responding. Many people forget communication is a bi-directional process.

THE IMPORTANCE OF TIMING

Timing and positioning of messages to match audience expectations is another key element. I remember a meeting with Corrado Passera, the then recently appointed CEO of the Olivetti group. We were discussing his contribution to an upcoming major customer event. We were going to gather together over six hundred representatives of our key customers, analysts and the media, from twenty-one countries, for a two-day conference. I wanted Corrado to conclude the conference with a personal exposition of his belief in Olivetti, its staff and customers. The style of the event was very much our customers talking about their business issues and how working with Olivetti had contributed to solving them. The objective was to give an opportunity for the rapid transfer of positive reputation around key stakeholders, from satisfied customers to other stakeholders present. Olivetti staff took very few of the speaking slots. We also invited key members of the analysts and media to freely mingle with the audience to show how confident we were in our organisation and its customer service and relationships.

We met in Corrado's office with an assembled group of interested parties. He began to tell me what he was going to say and when. To my horror I realised he wanted to give an aggressive and upbeat opening to the event, in effect stamping his mark clearly on the event and the organisation. But in the current situation this was neither useful nor relevant – Olivetti's reputation had been recently battered by a quick succession of CEO changes from Carlo De Benedetti to Francesco Kao and then to Corrado Passera. One more emphatic new leader was one too many. I felt that this surface noise masked the steady, competent and effective service Olivetti was giving to its customers around the world, despite the top management turmoil. We wanted to show to our stakeholders what our customers thought about us. The Olivetti relationship with its key banking and government customers was close and trusting. Giving them the opportunity to tell this to the assembled stakeholder audience would, we hoped, roll back some of the negative feelings that recent events had produced. The press and analysts were the key consumers of this message. Our customers already knew that we had performed business as usual throughout the turmoil. We wanted Corrado to save his powder for the final speech of the event. His words would have been confirmed and reinforced by the presentations from our customers during the event. If he spoke at the beginning we suspected most of the media would leave early, once they had footage and comments from him.

Corrado is an astute manager. Once he saw the logic and theme of the event, how the audience was made up and what they were expecting he was happy to play this role and deliver the final critical presentation of the event. Timing is vital when you communicate; the right thing at the wrong time is never half right but may be wholly wrong.

THE KEY COMMUNICATORS IN THE ORGANISATION AND THEIR ESSENTIAL QUALITIES

One of the ways organisations develop very positive reputations is through the communication skills of their leaders. Agilent has been a consistent member of *Fortune* magazine's 'Top one hundred companies to work for' and appears again in the survey published in 2003. Having a great relationship with your staff is very useful in time of crisis and downsizing.

A study of 18 years' worth of downsizing data by Wayne Cascio, a business school professor at the University of Colorado at Denver, found that while large staff redundancies may help raise share prices for a couple of years, they usually do not lead to greater profits. When expenses drop, revenue also tends to drop. The reduced workforce has to cope with what organisational behaviourists call survivor syndrome. This is characterised by anger, fear, anxiety, frustration, and decreased risk taking. 'Just when you need employees to take risks to turn the organisation around, they take to the trenches,' says David Noer, an employment consultant in Greensboro, N.C. 'You end up with a double loss.'

Agilent couldn't afford survivor syndrome when Hewlett Packard spun off the organisation in November 1999 to focus on PCs and computer equipment. Agilent was left with technologies that were the vital elements of a communications and networking infrastructure but which the general public never saw and would not understand if they did. To get out of its current recession, Agilent needed employees motivated enough to invent great products and give great service but it needed less of them.

Ned Barnholt is the CEO who runs Agilent. When Barnholt chats with employees, which he does frequently, he is Ned to them. Calling him 'Mr. Barnholt' would be very strange for his employees. His relaxed and consistent communications has maintained a high level of staff motivation and energy despite layoffs and the long fight to profitability and Agilent has maintained its reputation as a great employer. When you are fighting to attract the best and the brightest this is an extremely valuable asset.

This relaxed and open communications style may not be achievable for every top executive. However trying to move executives appropriately in this direction is shown to pay dividends. Communication style is also culturally dependent so the very informal US management approach may not necessarily play well in other countries, but motivated staff are far more willing to embrace change if they fully understand why it is necessary. Investing in your ability to explain and communicate the *how* and *why* is vital.

Virgin has proven to be successful in over 150 different businesses. The core of this success is Richard Branson's consummate ability to communicate. But it was not always like that and Richard did not breeze through school. He is dyslexic, which has made his life very tough at times, for example when he had to memorize and recite word for word in public. He was convinced he was rated lowly on the standard IQ tests because they measure abilities where he was weakest. These tests and his school failed to recognise Richard's most important talent, the ability to connect with people, and to communicate. 'It all comes down to people,' he remarked in an interview with David Sheff of Forbes. 'Nothing else even comes close.' He writes a chatty letter to all Virgin employees once a month and invites them to write or call him with their problems, ideas and dreams. They do and the Virgin success story continues.

ENSURE YOUR EXECUTIVES PRESENT THE BEST IMAGE OF YOUR ORGANISATION

All executives who give presentations to conferences and seminars need to be trained to deliver consistent and relevant messages. From the evidence produced by ITSMA this is one of the key sources of information for many buyers. Regular training is vital to ensure that you presenters are technically able to present and that they have a consistent set of messages that cover your organisation's strategy, offer, focus and competitive differentiation. Often understanding what the organisation's story is on these issues is left to a process of osmosis with no regular or formal training for people who are highly influential in forming the organisation's reputation. Considering the impact this type of communication has on your reputation, not having an ongoing plan to consistently inform and train your key corporate presenters is unnecessarily risky.

Companies invest effort and energy in gaining their ISO (International Standards Organisation) quality mark. They write the quality manual. Everyone is required to read it and understand it. When an inspector asks questions they should give the right standard answer as per the manual. They have to show a knowledge and adherence to the relevant process. So why do we often fail to train our key presenters to represent our organisation and its values effectively?

- Training the stock team is essential if you want to gain the ISO quality mark.
- Training your key presenters is vital if you want to develop and protect your reputation in the long term.

So how should we train these people? Give them the organisation's standard presentation and ask them to read it, memorise it and use it? Well of course you could do that and it may give some minor improvements in consistency of messages. But it will not improve their ability to communicate and achieve the empathy necessary to motivate their audiences positively. Hearing a presentation from a 'wooden' presenter obviously delivering the standard corporate pitch with little enthusiasm or expertise can be a very boring experience. I get very annoyed when people bore me, don't you?

Here we have a clear need for a training programme which works with each individual to develop a style that allows them to be both relaxed and effective.

Gavin Fenn-Smith, partner in the consultancy group Beasyousay, believes that such training programmes should try to give life skills as well as relevant business skills. So if, for example, effective presentation skills can help Joan in her local dramatics society activities or John's aspirations in local politics then you have a far higher level of motivation and attention. Beasyousay works with leaders of organisations to design, develop and execute innovative and practical strategies to engage with their employees during times of major change. Gavin argues that if you want to ensure your staff perform more often in the way you would like them to, they need to be well trained. They also need some higher motivation for any training initiatives other than the thought of doing a great job. Beasyousay, who specialise in major change programmes have found this to be a highly effective way of ensuring the training sticks.

Staff training is one of those chicken and egg issues for management. 'We have a higher staff turnover and lower customer satisfaction than we would like to have. This derives largely from our staff's lack of understanding of best practice and quality principles. This leads us to have lower sales figures and margins than we need to grow the business. In turn this means we do not have the time or money to train our staff.'

Effective management needs to find ways to break this cycle and make the investment necessary albeit maybe in a step-by-step way.

How do you manage who presents at conferences and other public events in your organisation? Do you have any form of control? Would you allow anybody in the organisation to reveal your financial results and answer questions on them? Many organisations do not have approval policies for staff involved in external speaking. Perhaps a policy of at least ensuring that senior managers are *licensed to present* may be one way. They must go through the training programme for presenters before they can represent the organisation as a speaker in external events. After all you would not send an engineer to repair a machine for which they have neither training nor the relevant parts, would you? Even senior managers should have a regular communications *certificate of roadworthiness*. Not to have a formal programme is to leave your organisation in the hands of good intentions alone.

We have not discussed the findings of our research yet. Ensuring you are already communicating effectively from the executive team and that your corporate communicators and presenters, wherever they are in the organisation, have the appropriate skills and information is a great start. It is the bedrock foundations on which to build your reputation management plan.

6 *Researching your Organisation's Reputation*

We have already travelled a long way together. We have discussed the differences between reputation and brand. We know what the available evidence says about the impact of reputation on our financial success and we have worked to identify who are the organisation's key stakeholders. We understand some of the critical scenarios that can seriously affect our reputation. We have identified key stakeholders as individuals and attributed them a loose weighting to establish who has the most impact. You have the buy-in of your senior management team and their commitment to initiate a research project.

But now comes the crunch time. Here is where we start to find out the facts and not simply opinions. Here is where the corporate ego can risk being dented. To identify the full picture of your reputation we need to start the research phase of our 360° analysis.

Building an effective questionnaire

The questionnaire needs to explore a consistent set of subjects across all groups so that a core sample can give you a 360° picture. Specific questions may be needed for specific groups but beware that the activity is not hijacked to become a customer satisfaction survey. The questions asked in this type of survey are usually quite different. The reputation survey should encourage open responses to open questions and the results will have the greater weight placed on the qualitative elements. In effect the survey is probing the emotional response to the organisation and its specific qualities, not simply gathering satisfied/quite-satisfied data. The objectivity of the questions is critical and having an external research organisation should avoid unconscious bias creeping in resulting in you finding what you want to hear and not the truth.

The development of the questionnaire is a significant step in the process. As it is developed the tendency may be to divert it into a multiple-choice optional questions set. When you set the available options via this type of survey you have some control over the answer given. This allows you to avoid highly critical or uncontrolled responses. But the key to this type of research is to have no control over the results, only to find the truth. The objective of the exercise should be kept firmly in your sights at all times. Your objective is to explore the emotional response of the subject to the reputation of your organisation in their industry and to understand their personal opinions. Having them rank, for instance, the minutiae of your offer and to rank it against the competition is not your objective. Neither is it to respond to a set of emotional trigger words with a cold or hot response. The objective is to have an open conversation around the issue of reputation and to gather some reference data points. However when you are researching your staff, if you decide to have a very wide sample, you may have to use a multiple-choice format for the non face-to-face or telephone interviews.

The importance of objectivity to reveal the whole truth

The research we are about to undertake is designed to find the truth about our reputation. But of course it will not do that. It will find a version of the truth. We know that when you research or survey a group of people then you create an artificial situation that in itself modifies the answers. Harry Beckwith in *The Invisible Touch* (Warner Books Inc., 2000) states, 'beware of research, people make terrible guinea pigs'. His advice is to rely more on anecdotal evidence that he says, 'comes from the real world'.

The trouble with reputation research is there is not much anecdotal evidence to go on. Your stakeholders do not usually tell you what they think about you, they only reveal their thoughts by actions and interaction with other stakeholders. One disparaging media story may be one journalist's angle and not a general view. The views of a major customer could be valid but it is very tough to initiate any form of change in your organisation based on a conversation over dinner. The research methods are designed to emulate as far as possible the normal way we pass on our views on an organisation's reputation – that is, during a conversation with a third party. The key quality of a good interviewer is to make the subject feel comfortable and begin to open up about their thoughts and feelings. The questionnaire is just a structure to hang the conversation around.

At the end of the day you will have a very useful version of the truth, but you will not have the whole truth and nothing but the truth. Imperfect perhaps, but I do not know of any better way to find out the required information.

The nature of the interview

A good interviewer will have structured questions in front of them and will use these questions in the appropriate order depending on the conversation but will ensure all of the aspects are covered. They will use secondary or exploratory questions to ensure they fully understand the responses they are given.

The ideal interview technique is to have two interviewers for every interview. One asks the questions and the other tries to take near verbatim notes. This prevents the loss of objectivity when the interviewer attempts, after the interview, to record what they have heard. It also allows the interviewer to concentrate on following the flow of the conversation and allows them to explore comments attentively. It is not easy to listen carefully and write extensive notes. After the interview the two versions of the interview can be balanced as the interviewers discuss what they have heard with very extensive notes in front of them. Having two people also helps to ensure greater objectivity, but this two-handed approach is obviously costly. It may well not be justified in anything other than the most critical interviews, for example, for stakeholders such as a major customer who you will interview face to face. This approach can allow the interview to not only fulfil its primary objective but also to explore other issues if time allows.

The length of interviews depends on the willingness of your stakeholders to be interviewed. Many executives receive multiple requests for interviews on a variety of subjects every week. They are forced to limit their time allotted to this activity. One of the options you may want to consider is offering an incentive to take part in the survey. Offering direct incentives could be considered a form of bribe but offering to donate to a charity an amount of money in the names of the people interviewed, for instance, is one way of making the interviewee feel that their efforts and time have helped someone else.

It is important to set the time you request for the interview to one that is reasonable and pragmatic. In my experience from twenty minutes to forty minutes for a telephone interview is adequate and from thirty minutes to an hour is acceptable for face-to-face interviewing.

The most satisfactory way to ensure candour from your subject is to promise complete anonymity. If you use internal research resources then this may be a challenge to be made credible. By promising that comments will never be attributed to an individual the subject is often much more willing to both spend more time and be very forthcoming about their opinions. I would suggest this type of research always demands a non-attributable approach. I have seen stakeholders eyes light up as they realise that what they say will never be reported back. They can say what they feel without let or hindrance. When you are interviewing in an attributable mode interviewees say things in a much more restrained way: 'quite happy' often 'means not very happy' and 'a little annoyed' means 'very annoyed'. However when you interview in a non-attributable mode some people take this as an opportunity to be very frank and may have a tendency to exaggerate slightly for effect. An astute interviewer will recognise the difference in most cases. Given our normal response to criticism, which is to soften its impact by making internal excuses, then perhaps a slight exaggeration of the problems and issues is healthy.

THE MOST EFFECTIVE QUESTIONS

The question set is an important issue. At the heart of a successful 360° study is a core set of questions that is asked of all respondents. These questions give you the ability to compare core groups and highlight differences between their perceptions of the organisation.

Every question set should begin with basic data collection. The name of the person interviewed may not be recorded because of your promise of anonymity but you will need to collect information about what they do and for which organisation. Some of the first questions will explore job role and organisation sector and size. For customers it is important to understand their role in the decision process, for contracts of the type your organisation is concerned with. Some details on purchase history such as purchases in the last year are also highly relevant. Obviously if the interviewee is not involved in the decision process and they have not bought this type of service in the last year, or other relevant time period, any comments they give are less significant in plotting the direct and immediate impact on your new business prospects. However their responses are useful corroborating information about your overall reputation. You might like to ask for some information about which media is most influential in providing information about companies and vendors of the type of service you are concerned with.

The question, 'are you involved in the decision process?' will trigger the interviewer to select the general reputation route or the more specific one including the RFP process after the section on basics data collection. Understanding the specific attitudes of people involved in this process is extremely important. Understanding how this process works in your specific industry and not relying on generic industry studies, if they exist, will give you an undoubted edge over your competition.

The RFP process route should seek to find out what influences the choice of organisations to bid for contracts and what are the key criteria for the final decision.

An example of what a question set might look like for a customer stakeholder interview is detailed below. Please do not consider this an instant survey kit. It is an example of the sort of questions you might want to ask one of the key stakeholder groups. It must be rewritten to cover your specific organisation's situation and industry. It is a question set that applies to an IT services provider. It is just intended as an example and as a very basic template.

Customer and prospect survey example

The interviewer will *not* give the multiple choices to the interviewee. They will ask the question and then interpret the answer using one of the options provided. If none of them fit reasonably they will note the answer as 'other' but also annotate the response form with the actual answer to allow the response form and data to be modified if the same answer is given by multiple respondents.

BASE DATA

Q   What is your organisation's primary business?

- [ ] Information technology
- [ ] Financial services (banking, insurance, investments)
- [ ] Government (regional or local, NOT education)
- [ ] Manufacturing
- [ ] Retailing
- [ ] Education
- [ ] Other services
- [ ] Other

Q   What is your organisation's approximate annual revenue (or total budget if a non-profit organisation)?

- [ ] Less than €1 million
- [ ] €1 million–€9.9 million
- [ ] €9.9 million–€100 million
- [ ] €100 million–€999 million
- [ ] €1 billion–€9.9 billion
- [ ] €10 billion–€20 billion
- [ ] Over €20 billion

Q   Has your organisation purchased services from the sponsor of this research in the last year?

- [ ] Yes
- [ ] No

Q   Has your organisation purchased similar services in the last year?

- [ ] Yes
- [ ] No

Q Which media do you read or watch normally?

Q Do you read Industry Analyst material or attend meetings and conferences. If so which ones?

Q What role did you personally play in the purchase process? Do you provide input to the purchase decision or do you authorise the purchase, personally or in a group?

☐ Provide input
☐ Authorise
☐ None

If the interviewee was involved in the purchase processes continue. Otherwise, go directly to the reputation assessment section.

BID PROCESS QUESTIONS

Q When you were in the process of selecting a service provider, how did you first learn about the service provider and its services?

Ask an open-ended question and do not prompt the answer. Use the list below to indicate the sources of information mentioned.

If they talk about a 'RFP or bid process' ask secondary questions to explore what they mean and how the process determines which vendors to invite to bid?

☐ Telephone marketing
☐ Other sales representative from the service provider
☐ Service delivery representatives
☐ Prior relationship with the service provider or the vendor has worked with us before
☐ Salesperson who sold us the product
☐ Direct mail or marketing literature
☐ Printed organisation newsletter
☐ Electronic organisation newsletter
☐ Organisation's web site
☐ Web searches
☐ Email from the organisation
☐ Advertisement – where?
☐ Article – where?
☐ Seminar or workshop
☐ Industry analysts
☐ Trade show
☐ Recommendation or reference – from?
☐ Overall knowledge of service provider's reputation or image
☐ Other

Q Rank the sources of information about potential suppliers in their order of importance from the list you gave in the last question.

☐ Telephone marketing
☐ Other sales representative from the service provider

- [ ] Prior relationship with the service provider or the vendor has worked with us before
- [ ] Salesperson who sold us the product
- [ ] Direct mail or marketing literature
- [ ] Printed organisation newsletter
- [ ] Electronic organisation newsletter
- [ ] Organisation web site
- [ ] Topical web searches
- [ ] Email from the organisation
- [ ] Advertisement – where?
- [ ] Article – where?
- [ ] Seminar or workshop
- [ ] Industry analysts (e.g. Gartner, IDC, Forrester)
- [ ] Trade shows
- [ ] Recommendation or reference – from?
- [ ] Overall knowledge of service provider's reputation or image
- [ ] Other

Q Who were the other service providers you were considering when you made this purchase? If no other service providers were considered why was that?

Q What criteria did you use to initially evaluate and then select the service providers that competed for your business?

Let's start with the criteria you used to initially evaluate the vendors. What would you say were the five most important factors to evaluate?

Note the five most important items. Use open-ended questions and do not prompt.

If they say 'the proposal' probe to find out what exactly it was about the proposal. For example, was it the qualities of the proposal document, the services included, the price, etc.

- [ ] Appropriate technical capabilities and expertise
- [ ] Prior relationship with the service provider or the vendor has worked with us before
- [ ] References
- [ ] Size of organisation
- [ ] Reputation of the vendor
- [ ] Geographic coverage
- [ ] Quality of sales person and sales presentation
- [ ] Quality of services personnel
- [ ] Lower price
- [ ] Quality of the proposal
- [ ] Reliability
- [ ] Responsiveness
- [ ] Breadth of offerings
- [ ] Financial stability
- [ ] No other alternative available
- [ ] Willingness to be flexible on pricing
- [ ] Cultural fit
- [ ] Industry or business knowledge
- [ ] Other

Q   What was the single most important reason you chose this vendor over any other?

Mark one only.

☐ Supplier/provider of product(s) to be supported
☐ Technical capabilities/expertise we required
☐ Prior relationship with the service provider or the vendor has worked with us before
☐ Reputation or references
☐ Size of support staff
☐ Timely access to or availability of support staff
☐ Geographic coverage
☐ Quality of sales person and sales presentation
☐ Quality of services personnel
☐ Web support capabilities/offerings
☐ Lower price
☐ Quality of the proposal
☐ Reliability
☐ Responsiveness
☐ Service level agreement (SLAs)
☐ Breadth of offerings
☐ Financial stability
☐ No other alternative available
☐ Willingness to be flexible on pricing
☐ Cultural fit
☐ Industry or business knowledge

Q   Which of the following people in your organisation would you say are decision makers or influencers for the purchase of these types of services?

Mark all that apply.

☐ Chief financial officer
☐ Chief executive officer
☐ Managing director or chief operating officer
☐ Chairman or president
☐ IT vice presidents or directors
☐ Business or functional vice presidents and directors
☐ Industry analysts
☐ Outside consultants
☐ Product vendors
☐ Other
☐ Don't know

Q   Who would you say has the ultimate sign-off authority?

Mark one only, please do not prompt.

☐ Chief financial officer
☐ Chief executive officer
☐ Managing director or chief operating officer
☐ Chairman or president

- [ ] IT vice presidents or directors
- [ ] Business or functional vice presidents and directors
- [ ] Industry analysts
- [ ] Outside consultants
- [ ] Product vendors
- [ ] Other
- [ ] Don't know

Q Which one of the following statements best describes your attitude toward your service vendor? Are you?

If they say they are committed due to a contract, ask them to answer the question as if the contract did not exist. If they have bought contracts from the organisation and another provider then ask the question for each of the contracts.

- [ ] Loyal to this service provider and would not switch.
- [ ] Would consider switching if something better came along.
- [ ] Actively looking for something better.
- [ ] Locked in because other vendors aren't any better.
- [ ] Locked in because there are no other companies that service my products.

Q What would be the number one reason you would switch from your incumbent service provider to a new service provider?

How likely would you be to switch from your existing service provider to a new provider under the following circumstances? Use a 5-point scale in which 1 = not at all likely and 5 = very likely.

- [ ] Your existing service firm makes a single costly error.
- [ ] Your existing service firm consistently falls below expectations.
- [ ] Your existing service firm is falling below expectations but has escalated the problem to their senior management to put it 'right'.
- [ ] A new firm offers to provide the same level of service for a lower price.
- [ ] A new firm provides a compelling return on investment analysis.
- [ ] A new firm can demonstrate via references and survey results a higher level of customer satisfaction.

REPUTATION QUESTIONS

This concludes the bid and contract process exploration section and now we move into the pure reputation section. If you have completed the first section many of the questions may have already been answered.

An astute interviewer will have noted the response and come back either with secondary questions to confirm the answer or will accept the answer already given. The order of the questions is not the critical factor. Having an open discussion on each of the topics and attempting to understand what the interviewee really feels about each subject is the most important objective. What are the words and comments that are repeated and emphasised?

Q What business would you say the organisation is in?

Q Based on what you know of the organisation, what products or services do you think it offers?

Q How likely are you to purchase this type of service over the next 12–18 months?

Q What values do you associate with the organisation? What words would you use to describe them?

Q In their industry, how would you rank them against the competitors you are aware of?

Q How would you describe the representatives of the organisation you have met?

Q How easy is the organisation to do business with?

Q What is that is the least pleasant part of they way they deal with you today? What irritates you about their behaviour?

Q What can you point to that are the best examples of good behaviour in the way they deal with you? What pleases you most?

Q Thinking about how you define good quality service, what would you say are the most important aspects of the services you intend to buy?

Q How would you summarise the organisations key strengths?

Q What about its weaknesses and, in particular, the areas would you like to see them improve upon?

Surveying staff

The survey sample is an example of a question set for a customer or a prospect. We have other groups to survey to complete the 360° analysis. The next key group to consider is your employees. They contribute more than any other to the evolution of your reputation. What they think and feel about the organisation influences everybody they come in contact with. You might try to deny this by assuming that they can put their feelings behind them and deal with every interaction with other stakeholders professionally. But your experience tells you that this is not so.

I live in a small village in Southern Sweden. It has around 1,000 inhabitants, about the same as a medium-sized organisation. The village businesses rely, to a great extent, on a seasonal influx of tourists mainly from within Sweden, Germany and Denmark. Ask a 'Skllingebo', an inhabitant of Skillinge, what they feel about their seasonal visitors and out come the 'don't mention the war' and '08' jokes (08 is the dialling code for Stockholm). The jokes are sort of friendly and usually not bitter or unpleasant and are fuelled, in part, by jealousy of the Saab- and Mercedes-driving visitors with their big-city confidence. Very few are genuinely accepted by the permanent residents, even after returning for many years as visitors. Among the residents are senior executives of companies, teachers, builders, fishermen, singers, artists, painters, and nurses – a veritable pot pourri of professions. They do not change when they go to work everyday. The same behaviour rules the day. They may assume a thin professional mask but beneath it all these same emotions guide the game.

If a key reason a customer buys is 'I get on well with your people' or 'I trust you to deliver', perhaps it does not hurt to know what your employees really think about your organisation. How well do they understand your customers and their needs and feelings? What is their perception of what matters most to your customers?

Groups achieve their greatest unity often when united against a common enemy. It helps to know if you have a common enemy. Let us hope it is not the management team or the customers. As we know emotions are catching and form the largest component of infectious history.

The heart of your organisation is its people. Taking a 'health check' on their emotions and attitudes is just as essential as a regular check up on your own heart. Their actions and behaviour have a profound impact on your corporate reputation.

- Are they sending the right messages to your customer consciously or unconsciously?
- Are they motivated to give great service?
- Are they in sympathy with the attitudes and beliefs of you customers?
- What do they feel about your customers?
- Do they understand what the organisation is trying to achieve and where it is going?

Are they well informed about its current status?

THE METHODS MAY BE SLIGHTLY DIFFERENT

Depending on how many and where your employees are located you can choose a variety of different research methods. Some of the options are face-to-face, telephone, email, postal and Web based. I would recommend that you ensure that the survey is anonymous and that a proportion of the interviews are conducted face to face by the same team that carried out the customer survey. You will find the most revealing data from the face-to-face interviews. A good interviewer will explore answers and follow relevant thoughts that may not be covered in the survey. This can help to expose issues that are not only impacting your reputation but also the effectiveness of your organisation.

The techniques you can use in the non face to face part of the employee survey is different in that you probably cannot use the very open ended questions that you have used with your customer base. The results will not mean very much without the ability to interpret the answers and the opportunity to ask additional questions. The responses derived from open questions will have many ways to be misunderstood and are not likely to provide very useful results.

The following survey is for an organisation in the IT service area. Again, it is intended merely as an example of what sort of questions you might ask. It is not a list of standard questions that you can use without redesigning it to cover your specific situation.

Employee survey example

Please complete the questionnaire in full and return it as soon as possible. Thank you for your participation.

Remember this is an anonymous survey and we do not need to know who you are. We value your opinions and thoughts. Please be frank and honest in your answers.

SECTION 1

Please complete these details in full. This will help us to analyse the results correctly.

Department:

Office or site based:

Length of service with the organisation:

Which location do you work from?

SECTION 2

Please answer all of these questions. Remember, there are no right or wrong answers; we are interested in your opinions only.

1   Which of these activities best describes the nature of the organisation's business? (Please tick all that apply.)

Cabling infrastructure ☐
Network management ☐
System integrator ☐
Consultancy ☐
Network infrastructure provider ☐
Value added reseller ☐
Network integrator ☐
Other please specify: ☐

2   What range of services does the organisation offer? (Please tick all that apply.)

PC maintenance ☐
Cabling infrastructure ☐
LAN services ☐
WAN services ☐
Virtual private networks ☐

Internet infrastructure ☐
Customer relationship management solutions ☐
E-commerce solutions ☐
Network security ☐
Web site design and management ☐
Internet service provider ☐
Network infrastructure and maintenance ☐
Telephony solutions ☐
Telephony support and maintenance ☐
Moves adds and changes ☐
Network fault response ☐
Storage area networks ☐
Fibre design and installations ☐
Other please specify: ☐

3 What words would you use to describe the organisation? (Please tick all that you think apply in the 'All' column, and then please select the one word that you think best describes the organisation and select it in the 'Best' column.)

Words	All	Best
Quality	☐	☐
Expensive	☐	☐
Communications	☐	☐
Cabling	☐	☐
Innovative	☐	☐
Dynamic	☐	☐
Hi-tech	☐	☐
Caring	☐	☐
Badly organised	☐	☐
Professional	☐	☐
Independent	☐	☐
Consultative	☐	☐
Bureaucratic	☐	☐
Flexible	☐	☐
Trustworthy	☐	☐
Honest	☐	☐
Inflexible	☐	☐
Transparent	☐	☐
Dedicated	☐	☐
Approachable	☐	☐
Listening	☐	☐
Team approach	☐	☐
Reliable	☐	☐
Well known	☐	☐
Reputable	☐	☐

4   To what extent do you agree or disagree with the following statements? (Please tick as appropriate.)

Statement	Strongly agree	Agree	Neither agree nor disagree	Disagree	Strongly disagree
The organisation has an excellent track record on cabling projects.	☐	☐	☐	☐	☐
The organisation has an excellent track record on networking projects.	☐	☐	☐	☐	☐
The organisation has an excellent track record on maintenance and outsourced projects.	☐	☐	☐	☐	☐
The organisation has excellent references and case studies from its previous clients.	☐	☐	☐	☐	☐
The organisation does not always deliver what it promises to customers.	☐	☐	☐	☐	☐
The organisation is known for its customer care and asks for feedback throughout a project.	☐	☐	☐	☐	☐
All of the organisation's technical staff have appropriate qualifications.	☐	☐	☐	☐	☐
The organisation can give clients assurance that deadlines will be met.	☐	☐	☐	☐	☐
The organisation only really cares about profits.	☐	☐	☐	☐	☐
The organisation can give clients assurance that they will stick to budget.	☐	☐	☐	☐	☐
The organisation can advise on security policies, conduct audits and complete action without using sub-contractors.	☐	☐	☐	☐	☐
The organisation has friendly and approachable staff.	☐	☐	☐	☐	☐
The organisation demonstrates a willingness to understand its clients' unique requirements.	☐	☐	☐	☐	☐
The organisation often makes mistakes with customer billing and invoicing.	☐	☐	☐	☐	☐
The organisation is one of the best companies to work for in this industry.	☐	☐	☐	☐	☐

5   How would you rate the following aspects of the organisation's business, in terms of whether they are better, the same, or worse than competitors in the market? (Please tick as appropriate.)

The organisation's business activities	Better	Same	Worse	Don't know
Setting organisational direction and strategy	☐	☐	☐	☐
Recruiting and developing staff	☐	☐	☐	☐
Building a strong brand in the market	☐	☐	☐	☐
Winning new clients	☐	☐	☐	☐
Building relationships with clients	☐	☐	☐	☐
Winning repeat business from existing clients	☐	☐	☐	☐
Delivering projects on time and to budget	☐	☐	☐	☐
Offering clients value for money	☐	☐	☐	☐
Delivering a consistent quality of service	☐	☐	☐	☐
Managing partners and suppliers	☐	☐	☐	☐
Using the latest and most appropriate technology	☐	☐	☐	☐
Managing and reducing costs	☐	☐	☐	☐
Negotiating good prices with suppliers	☐	☐	☐	☐
Designing and launching new services for clients	☐	☐	☐	☐
Managing and sharing knowledge within the organisation	☐	☐	☐	☐
Making a profit	☐	☐	☐	☐
Growing the organisation	☐	☐	☐	☐
Investing in staff training and development	☐	☐	☐	☐
A wide range of service offerings	☐	☐	☐	☐

6   Which competitors were you thinking of when completing the previous question?

7   How would you rate the following attributes of the organisation's service, in terms of attractiveness to our customers? Please answer as you think our customers would answer these questions. (Please tick as appropriate.)

The organisation's service attributes activities	Strongly agree	Agree	Neither agree nor disagree	Disagree	Strongly disagree
Well known organisation with a good reputation	☐	☐	☐	☐	☐
Well trained and technically qualified staff	☐	☐	☐	☐	☐
Commitment to deliver on time and on budget	☐	☐	☐	☐	☐
The relationship with the organisation's staff	☐	☐	☐	☐	☐
Works hard to build relationships with clients	☐	☐	☐	☐	☐
Has done successful projects for us before	☐	☐	☐	☐	☐
Offering value for money	☐	☐	☐	☐	☐
Delivers a consistent quality of service	☐	☐	☐	☐	☐
Has good partners and suppliers	☐	☐	☐	☐	☐
Uses the latest and most appropriate technology	☐	☐	☐	☐	☐
Is well known in the industry	☐	☐	☐	☐	☐
Negotiates good prices with suppliers	☐	☐	☐	☐	☐
Is designing and launching new services	☐	☐	☐	☐	☐
Has a good reputation	☐	☐	☐	☐	☐
Is a profitable organisation	☐	☐	☐	☐	☐
Is a growing organisation	☐	☐	☐	☐	☐
Invests in staff training and development	☐	☐	☐	☐	☐
A wide range of service offerings	☐	☐	☐	☐	☐

8   Please pick one of the attributes in the list above you think our customers value the most highly in their relationship with the organisation.

Thank you for completing the survey; please use the pre-paid envelope provided to return your answers to the Marketing Department.

The importance of patience while the research team assesses the results

When the results of both the customer and prospects surveys and your own staff are complete you have the major pieces of the 360° puzzle in place. Other groups you may want to survey such as industry and financial analysts, partners and the media are best covered in the same way as with customers via telephone or face-to-face interviews.

When the first responses are in then you need to give the team analysing the results space and do not expect interim reports or snap feedback. They need thinking time to digest and cross analyse the results. They need to sift through the responses to select quotes that epitomise the reactions of your stakeholders to your reputation. These are always more powerful than statistics or general observations.

You need to keep the executive team off the backs of the research group until they can complete their work. Any comments you give now, based on any preliminary findings, will only serve to pressure them towards the results you want, not towards a balanced and honest result.

The research findings will help to shape the next phase. The media and industry analysts mentioned in the research carried out to date are likely to be some of the most influential on your reputation and hence should be the next targets for interviews.

These stakeholder groups will provide the majority of the substance of your data. It is tempting to stop here and consider this is enough. But we know the stakeholder groups influence each other. If you fail to research the whole circle of stakeholders you will not truly understand the issues. You will not be able to design and implement an effective management programme. Without the whole picture you risk making some wrong assumptions.

'Do not spoil the ship for a ha'porth of tar!'

Including your partners in the process

If you work extensively with partners then comments on their reputations may also have been received. If you work closely with partners your reputations will in many ways be intertwined. Perhaps you should wait until you have finished surveying them before deciding whether to reveal what other stakeholders think about your partners. The decision to reveal research data to them should be considered carefully. If they do not understand and accept the relevance of the data then you may do more harm than good by revealing it. You might consider inviting them to have your outside consultants provide the same sort of executive briefing meeting as your own team undertook and then at the end reveal the findings that are relevant to them. This way you are more certain they will understand the data and how it was gathered. Sharing information without understanding the research project in detail could lead to many misunderstandings and no positive steps being taken by the partner to act on the findings.

You might consider bringing your partners into the research project from the beginning. The danger with this is that it could make the project unwieldy and difficult to manage. There are many ways the process can be derailed so think very carefully about adding one more.

7 *The Results of your Research*

Well now we have the results of our research. We know the realities, for good or bad. How should we put this new knowledge to good use? The actions required will of course very much depend on what you have found. If the feedback you have from all groups is positive and appropriate then well done, perhaps you do not need to do anything at all. However I doubt that this will be the case. We all know that we are not perfect people or organisations. Even perfect companies delivering perfect products and services can be misunderstood. So more likely than not you will find areas that you need to work on.

The areas you may find stakeholders are less than happy with should prompt you to make changes of process and behaviour. This will require that every one involved 'buys into' the necessary changes.

Common issues the research may have revealed

- Often differences exist between what your customers and prospects value most highly in your organisation and what your staff believes to be your more appealing attributes. The danger with this is that you will be sending the wrong messages to your external stakeholders. Each time they emphasise the wrong attributes they create a barrier between themselves and your customers and prospects. This is not helpful in building long-term close and trusting relationships.
- Your organisation may have an arrogant, insular or over-confident culture that irritates some customers.
- You could be lacking in confidence and resorting to unjustified hyperbole in your communications.
- Staff may be low in motivation and trust in your organisation, which of course spreads like the bubonic plague to your other stakeholders.
- There may be weak or broken processes that provide poor customer service.
- You may have disjointed or weak external communications, which prevents stakeholders from understanding who you are and what value you bring.
- You could have brand recognition issues.
- Poor public relations management could be allowing negative media comments to affect your reputation or you may not be capitalising on the opportunities the media presents you.
- You may not be communicating effectively with influential industry analysts.
- Your sales process may have skill, competence or organisational problems.
- Perhaps you have lost touch with the evolving demands of your customers and market.
- The organisation may have a weak value proposition.

The problems and issues that this research may reveal are potentially wide ranging. Let us hope you do not find the last three in the list above as these are probably some of the more challenging to resolve. Whatever the issues revealed building the right levels of energy and commitment to resolving them is the next vital step.

To progress this chapter further we will discuss in more depth some of the issues listed above and methods of effecting performance improvements.

Customer and staff expectation mismatch

Often it is found that the employee's views of key and highly valued attributes of your organisation are different from those of your customers. Many surveys I have seen show high staff valuations of attributes such as global, broad offering and high technical skills. Now why is that? It does not take a genius to work out these are ego values. Either this is the reflection of the corporate ego or of the staff themselves. 'We are a global organisation offering a wide range of offerings with the most innovative technologies.'

While in contrast the customer believes you have a highly competent niche offer, that they have selected from you in the one country they operate within. And actually you are not bleeding edge technology and that is one of the reasons they chose you. They like the qualities of your people but find a lot of your corporate messaging pompous and not credible. You are not a centre stage supplier but you do what you do quite well.

The problem with this is that you are creating differences with your customers and prospects. Every time you repeat the corporate mantras you reveal to them that you do not really understand them. Individual members of your staff may drop the misjudged corporate messaging but this in turn is telling your stakeholders that you may have people who know how to communicate with them but that your leadership does not really understand its market and customers. It is a sort of half success but not a good launching place for a long-term, close and trusting business relationship between the two organisations. This sort of mismatch is usually the fault of ambitious corporate mission statements that are being echoed by staff. Modifying your messaging and explaining to your organisation what your customers and prospects value most highly about your behaviour is a useful start.

Marshall McLuhan wrote in 1967 that he believed that in multimedia communication, how the message arrives is often as important as what the message actually is. The two are entangled. Your own messaging is entangled in the whole multimedia organisational experience you deliver to your customers and stakeholders. You can claim greatness but if you cannot support it in reality then it will not be believed. In reputational speak we should rephrase this as 'your reputation is the organisation'.

If your messaging fails the credibility test then you may need to work on some key behavioural changes. Corporate lack of self-confidence is often exampled by the over-blown messaging. We humans boast to show that we are really powerful and significant when we think others do not sees us that way. Nine times out of ten our boasting is not believed. In children it is seen as a phase we are going through and easily forgiven. In companies it is seen as a sign of lack of self-confidence and places you as a third tier or a desperately striving player.

Forget your own messaging for a moment and think about some of the organisations you deal with:

- Do you believe their messaging?
- Is it supported by your experience?
- How do you feel about this?
- How have you received and reacted to their corporate messages?
- Do any of your first tier suppliers or your most admired companies resort to corporate hyperbole?

Corporate messaging should be based on the real you on your best day

Your corporate messaging might need revisiting. The research will have given you masses of vital information as to how you can modify it to be more believable and closer to your delivered reality. Charles Doyle of Accenture expressed his belief of what constitutes the best corporate messaging position as 'Accenture on its best day'; in other words, a credible and achievable position but still it is aspirational. He also went on to emphasise that positioning must be aligned with business strategy and is the context for all marketing messages and communications. It should be reflected in everything that is said and done by everybody in the organisation.

Derek Hardman, Marketing Director for Fujitsu Services says, 'Does the brand build the company or the company build the brand? Your brand and messaging should come from the real qualities of the experiences you are able to deliver. Not from a wild dream that you hope you can push your organisation towards.'

We must rethink how we express our qualities and develop a more believable and relevant set of messages. The messages we have developed need to move us forward and our stakeholders with us. It should not leave them behind in disbelief.

Industry analysts

Did you find that the industry analysts knew very little about you and what your organisation is really capable of? Let us hope this is the case rather than they have already pigeonholed you as a minor league player. If the former is the case then improving their perceptions of you is straightforward. The major issue to overcome is indifference. However if the analysts have a less than useful view of you organisation a lot more patient and persistent work will be required. In many markets the analysts are very influential so investing time in them is well worthwhile. I have included a whole chapter on analyst management later so we do not need to consider this in detail here.

The media

The media covers a wide range of interests. They range from the specialist press (that is, industry-focused media that usually has highly knowledgeable reporters who in many ways are similar to industry analysts) to the national press and television. Your research is less likely to have given results from the national media. They normally only want to hear about you when the news is big. But the local media and specialist media are more likely to have formed opinions about your organisation. Those opinions can be identified using our classic research techniques. Armed with this knowledge we can build a plan to overcome and modify any less helpful parts of their perceptions.

Your objectives with the media need to be carefully assessed. Many American based organisations issue press releases as a way of attempting to influence their stock price. They issue long fact rich releases containing marketing messages. These then are reported on the systems investors use to track the latest equities information. If this is your objective then do not be surprised if this is the only place your news is reported.

This type of release does not work well in Europe if you actually want to be reported in the media. Time pressed journalists want news releases they can cut and paste without extensive editing. Hence too much marketing hype spoils that objective. They want material written in such a way that it can be cut at almost any point and still make sense. Most US news releases cannot be directly used without being rewritten and hence unless the contents are must haves they are rarely used by journalists. But managing the media is not about firing out the occasional press release and wondering why nobody prints it. It is far more about a long-term patient campaign to gain consistent favourable mentions in your key target media.

The key to managing the media is to have a media management plan. Whether you are using an external public relations group to help you or internal resources the plan is the vital element. One of the most effective weapons in your media toolkit is your top executives. We have already discussed the need to give your senior executive team communications training which includes how to deal with the media. Improving their knowledge of the requirements of the media and the impact they can have upon your organisation should at least make them more careful and respectful when dealing with them.

CRISIS MANAGEMENT PLAN

A crisis can arise from a number of negative and positive events. Its distinguishing features are that it is a very significant issue for the organisation and it has arisen suddenly. These sorts of event can seriously damage your reputation so having a well rehearsed crisis management plan pays handsome dividends.

The plan should cover issues such as:

- Who are the members of the crisis committee and which of them is your designated spokesperson.
- Widely understood rules of behaviour which dictate that all other people in the company should say nothing unless they are guided to do so by a crisis committee. Even the CEO should obey this rule.
- Documented rules of disclosure of information taking particular notice of issues such as insider trading and the timing of the release of information if you are a publicly traded company.
- The composition of the committee and procedures to call it together quickly and remotely if necessary.
- The composition of an expert panel that could be consulted on particular issues for advice and guidance.
- Last but certainly not least is a process to escalate potential issues to be watched and influenced so they do not turn into PR crises.

Every company should have such a crisis plan if only to designate who is allowed to speak to the media and what approvals they need to obtain for what they can say. You should also rehearse it from time to time to see if it works.

LONG-TERM INFLUENCE

From your research you will have a good idea of which media matters most to you. You should build a plan to influence this media to report the messages you believe are helpful to the positive evolution of your reputation. The public relations team you are using be it internal or external should identify each of the key media and within these organisations the individuals who matter.

A long-term plan to influence them should include ensuring you know what they will be covering well in advance. Many specialist media have regular or pre-planned issues they are going to cover. The schedule for these is often published six months or more in advance. By approaching the journalist at the appropriate time to offer information, interviews, white papers on the subject and access to customers if relevant you can help the journalist to do their job. In the process you can expect to be more positively mentioned. Timing your offer of assistance is critical, not too early and not too late. A good PR management team will learn by experience what is the appropriate timing for each publication and journalist. The same comment applies to the industry analysts who publish regular or pre-programmed reports.

You should be regularly scanning your key media to identify key issues that you know the journalist or the particular media are interested in and find ways of placing your stories and information. If you are very astute and you have someone in your organisation with the appropriate intellect and discipline then they can be positioned as an industry expert. The media like to have an informal panel of such people to call for comment on issues or simply to understand the implications of a particular piece of news. Having a recognised industry expert is a very effective way of gaining positive mentions that position your organisation as the experts in the field. However, I have seen some occasions when the expert is handicapped by internal jealousy from senior managers who believe they should be the people in the media's eyes. This role can leave you exposed. Particularly when you consider the issue of the normal human reaction we have to people we know, and have worked with closely, now being seen by the media as experts. Often it is difficult to overcome our familiarity with both their strengths and weaknesses. It can be characterised by the eternal problems associated with trying to be a prophet in your own land. The role of your media management team must be to explain the value of the expert and establish it as an objective of your media plan. They should also protect and support their expert as much as possible in return for their agreement to play the corporate line and not to try to go too far with a personality cult.

The closer and more supportive you can be to the key media the more likely they are to report your issues and organisation positively.

Customer-facing staff

Nice messaging changes not very much, of course. The key next step is to turn messages into reality. The customer-touch points, where customer and organisation get up close and personal, will probably be key areas of interest.

THE SALES PROCESS

Does your sales force have the right attitude and skills? Did you find that your sales team is not considered by your customers and prospects to be consultative and influential? Well changing your sales team's approach is like changing the wheel of a car while it is moving. Definitely this should be well thought out and carefully managed if you do not want to badly disrupt business generation activities. I have seen companies approach this problem by a process of 'mind setting' courses. Depending on the research findings the content will differ and a number of elements may need to be included to address the issues fully.

You may wish to consider 'quick think' sessions at which the market, its trends and customers' evolving needs are thoroughly discussed. Your organisation's role and relative position is compared and contrasted via strengths, weaknesses, threats and opportunity analysis. SWOT analysis is not rocket science but if it is applied with discipline it can be very useful.

In the process your sales team should also be introduced to your research findings. This helps them to put a mirror up to themselves to see how they behave from their customer's eyes. The question set should have asked questions about the sales team if you have a direct selling sales organisation.

The RFP and bid process could be a focus of the sessions if you are not regularly carrying out this training already. Any research you have should be used to ensure the team understands the process as well as is possible with the takeaway mission to research their own account's processes in detail.

Account planning might also be a part of the mind setting courses, reinforcing existing account planning processes or introducing it for the first time if you are not doing this already.

Industry issues and background information are also vital to build their knowledge and allow them to be more consultative and advisory towards their customers and prospects.

Many organisations having recognised that the research has revealed a sales force weakness have combined the introduction of a long-term mind-setting programme with a weeding of the patch. Under performing sales people, as assessed by their sales performance figures and the results of their efforts on the courses, are progressively removed from the team. This process can be painful but may be the only way to make changes of attitude and behaviour stick in the longer term. I have even seen an organisation's top performing sales person removed because they were a bad example of the old ways and attitudes and because they were not prepared to change. It takes a brave management team to do this but it can be the only way to break old habits and move in another direction.

How you motivate your sales team is a core decision. Some organisations adopt the sports team approach. 'We are the best the most dynamic and the most talented team. We can do it! Let's get out there and kill them!' In the early seventies Xerox had one of the best trained and highly motivated sales teams in the business world. They were a macho, hard drinking and hard partying bunch. They believed they were the best and they believed that Xerox's success relied solely on them. But of course it did not. Xerox was successful mainly because of patent protection and when this protection went away Japanese competitors responded with product innovation, purchase options, price performance advantages and more sympathetic sales approaches from their resellers. Xerox's business quickly started to have problems. Customers were very happy to get rid of this cocky and arrogant sales force with its high priced products. Their attitude may have been overly aggressive but their sales skills were derived from probably the best training programme of its type. The knife in the hands of a thug can kill but in the hands of a surgeon it can remove the most life-threatening tumour.

It is not easy to be a sales person. Your ego is bruised almost daily as customers and prospects do not do what you need them to do in order for you to reach your targets. All the bravado disguises the hard emotional knocks sales people have to deal with almost every day. Organisations hold out big carrots to motivate them to achieve more and yet more – like rats on a treadmill with the cheese just out of reach. They create environments that almost take them out of the real world with awards, clubs and status based solely on sales achievements. When the heat is turned up high it is very tempting for the sales team to indulge in short-term deception to achieve this month's numbers. A customer may be oversold or promised concessions further down the road. But what is the effect on your reputation of these cumulative deceptions?

You need to train and nurture your sales team with '*real food*' not just give them prizes and tell them they are brilliant. They need something of value to sell, and training to be effective in helping the customer to select your products or services. Then they need good incentives. Above all they should reflect your values and standards.

One of the core issues with managing a sales team, particularly a successful sales team, is who is managing whom? Often the sales team manages the organisation and not vice versa. Rather like Clement Atlee's policy of appeasement before World War Two, delaying firm action only makes things very much worse in the longer term. If you want to manage your organisation and of course your reputation the executive team must have all the tools at its disposal, and a renegade sales force is not going to help.

But bare in mind it is equally unfair to ask a sales team to sell a poor product or service, which does not meet the demands of your customers. The response often is to whip the galley slaves harder because all that is needed is simply much more effort. This may be the wrong approach. If your value proposition is more myth than reality and is not appreciated by your customer base then this should have been revealed by your research. Still however the signs may be interpreted as 'it's not being explained properly'. Companies sometimes think that having a good value proposition statement is the problem. When the problem *is* the value proposition!

Let's hope your core issue is messaging and sale force training reengineering your value proposition demands much more radical action.

TOUCH POINT MAPPING

If you have found you are not as easy an organisation to deal with as you thought you were, then trying to map out the critical points of interaction with your organisation can help you to understand where the customer experiences difficulties. You may decide to carry out touch point mapping directly after you have the research results, to understand them better, or as a part of your ongoing reputation management plan. Using a matrix, like the one in Figure 4 below, can help to put a structure around such customer interactions. By customer of course I mean any interaction with existing or potential customers. The same process can be applied to any other stakeholder group to understand how the process of interaction with your organisation works.

This approach is similar to process mapping used in quality improvement programmes. The process mapping technique involves the creation of flowcharts, which illustrate the individual steps involved in a given process, and hence pinpoint where problems arise and identify areas that could be improved. Mapping is particularly useful for spotting 'bottlenecks', points in a process where delays may occur. By taking a close look at the process in this way, it may even be possible to remove unnecessary steps entirely.

In touch point mapping we need to focus on how the customer is affected by the process. How their impressions and feelings are impacted by the touch-points of the process. You can also try to review the whole process at the same time from a process mapping point of view. But remember we are trying to improve our reputation by ensuring the customer is dealt with in a way they find appropriate and satisfying. Process improvements are only a by-product of touch point mapping. The correct approach is at all times to try to see the process from the customer's viewpoint. To attempt to ignore why your organisation currently does it this way. A naive approach to looking at yourself from the outside can bring huge benefits in terms of understanding what you are actually doing to your customers. Customers are often not prepared to tell you why they are disappointed in your organisation they simply buy elsewhere.

Firstly we need to look at the physical evidence such as documentation, time to respond for telephone calls etc. Then, what actions and information are required by the customers to initiate a reaction from you?

The 'on stage' customer visible actions are considered next and then the 'back stage' actions which are directly associated with the particular touch point follow.

The processes that support responses to a particular customer interaction complete the map.

What you are trying to understand is how it actually happens not what the quality manual says should happen. The approach needs to be naive but investigative, looking at a number of randomly selected examples to follow the process from initiation to conclusion. Discussing the process with individual customers may also help to shed light on how the process works in reality.

This form of mapping often reveals issues of systems, training or understanding of customer requirements. Sometimes a bad customer experience is the result of inflexible IT systems that do not allow the customer to interact with the organisation in the way that suits them. This may lead to well-intentioned attempts to mask inflexible systems with

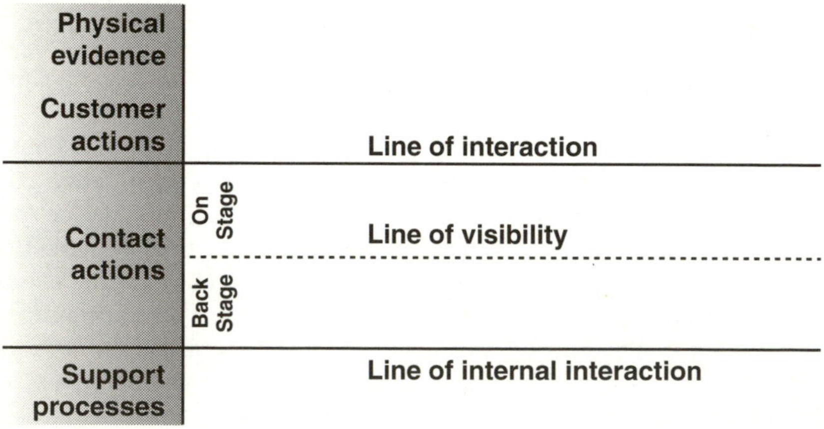

Figure 4   Touch point mapping

labour intensive activity that presents information in the way the customer would like to see it. But this may break down when overloaded or under resourced.

This process may also reveal a mismatch between your marketing claims and reality. The 'listening' bank syndrome is an example. What was thought to happen by marketing may not happen in fact. This can be either because the service delivery team are not motivated or resourced sufficiently to carry out the activity with which they have been tasked. It is very easy for marketing to become detached from the realities of the process of delivery of products and services. The phrase 'responsible for everything but with the authority to do very little' cover the realities of many marketers position. It is easy for marketing to say, 'we designed the service to provide the customer with what we think they want but it is not our job to deliver it!' But as the representative of the customer inside the organisation it is their role to ensure that what is agreed will be delivered, is in fact delivered. And if it is not, to escalate it up to the level of management necessary to ensure that what you claim is a reality. Or you must change your marketing claims to match reality.

We see many advertisements that make claims that stretch our credibility: the Diners' Club promise that, 'no door will remain closed to you' when you have a Diners' club card. How do you react to this sort of messaging? Perhaps it is wise to test this sort of messaging to see whether your target audience's credibility is not being stretched too far.

The 'who sold you this' syndrome is equally dangerous to your reputation. If sales and service are not in harmony and service believes sales are overselling or selling the wrong things they can be tempted to say this to the customer. Touch point mapping should reveal this as a problem that needs urgent attention. Customers often consider service delivery staff to be more believable than sales staff. Their comments can do real damage to your corporate reputation. Even if it is true they should not say, 'who sold you this' but instead escalate the problem through appropriate channels repeatedly until it is fixed.

Your research into customer attitudes may show that they do not receive enough information during the process of an enquiry or issue. One of the most frustrating things a human being can experience is to be ignored. A failure to respond and recognise that an enquiry has been made and is being dealt with is in my view a capital crime. Being by nature an impatient animal I want to be assured you have received my message. I do not think I am unique in this personal attribute.

Often staff who manage the customer interaction are focused on their internal issues and fail to understand what impact their actions have on customers. I have seen excellent results when customers are invited to talk with the people who deliver service. When they understand the *why and how* it can profoundly change their behaviour.

Touch point mapping is a whole subject in itself and a powerful way of truly understanding how your organisation works as seen from your customer's eyes. Linking this to your reputation research gives you the evidence necessary to institute kaizen type improvements. Hopefully this is going to be what you need to do and not rethink things from the ground up.

It may not be easy to implement the changes of approach that your touch point mapping may have revealed.

- Staff may feel apathetic and believe that there is no need for change, particularly if the business is already perceived to be successful. There may be room for improvement in a given process, but the employee attitude may be 'it isn't broken, so why fix it?'

- Even if everyone involved with the business agrees with the need for change, the staff may see a change of approach as overly elaborate and excessive. They may indeed be very cynical about change.
- Change is a big commitment; and there may not be enough resources to have people trained, or even to take time out to review the business effectively. The response, 'we are too busy to make changes', if true, would signal real problems for the future of the business.

The keys to removing these obstacles are effective communication and a 'walking the talk' behaviour from management. They must make appropriate resources available to implement change. Equally uncompromising action must be taken towards people who block change or pay it only lip service. The carrot and the stick whilst standing on a burning platform is the image you should bear in mind. If this visual imagery becomes any more complicated we are going to collapse into a farce so I will not develop it any further. Suffice to suggest that we must:

- Build an urgent reason for change – a burning platform, more comfortable to move from it than remain.
- Communicate, communicate and communicate effectively the good reasons for change and its benefits to the organisation.
- Explain what needs to be done specifically.
- Provide adequate resource to effect change.
- Reinforce change by management example.
- Remove the obstacles to change.

8 *Building and Implementing the Plan*

Let us now consider the key steps in building a plan based on your research findings and any subsequent investigations you may have carried out such as touch point mapping.

Is the CEO leading the pack?

The degree of responsibility felt by the CEO for the current status of the organisation's reputation, as revealed by the research, may well have a strong bearing on his or her reaction. If the chief executive officer is not prepared to put his or her shoulder behind any plan then you have a potentially terminal problem. If a careful buy in process has been followed and both senior and middle management have accepted the results then the acceptance by the CEO of a plan for change will be easier to achieve.

It will be critical to find ways for the CEO to feel ownership for the findings and for the resultant actions. Small incremental steps in building that commitment can often pay dividends. An early small step is perhaps a letter from the CEO to all who contributed to the research sent right after the data collection is finished and before the findings are known might be one way to progressively build a commitment.

THE LETTER

The CEO's letter should of course acknowledge that individual comments are not known and that their contribution has been important to the organisation to ensure it keeps in tune with its major stakeholders and that the findings will be a key element in the organisation's ongoing planning process. The letter should not promise too much as in doing so you signal that major issues have been found and to promise their prompt resolution may not be achievable in the timescales that customers and other stakeholders expect. Now is certainly the time to promise not so much but to deliver far more.

In a flotilla organisation the CEO's buy-in will signal whether the project is significant or can be ignored. Similar highly visible symbols of commitment are critical. By a 'flotilla' organisation I am referring to those that are driven by dominant management that expects the people to follow orders with little discussion. In this type of organisation you often see people striving to gain advancement by showing they are the most zealously committed to management.

LEADERSHIP IS VITAL

Richard Christou, the CEO of Fujitsu Services was prepared to lead the charge on the issue of reputation. Fujitsu Services was born out of Fujitsu's acquisition of UK headquartered ICL. ICL had been going through a period of difficulty in its change of focus from being a hardware and software organisation to a services led organisation. This had entailed a comprehensive programme of reorganisation, re-streaming and rationalisation, a polite way of saying lay offs. The ICL brand had suffered from a second tier market perception with a very UK centric business. The move to adopt their parents global brand under the Fujitsu name gave it the chance to migrate the good reputation ICL held, with its UK customers, into a brand that was emphatically global and first tier. During the height of the re-branding phase Richard chose a Gartner conference to remind everybody that despite the fervour of re-branding he had not lost sight of the tight linkage between delivering what you promise, which builds reputation, and ultimately success in terms of customer loyalty.

This feet on the ground approach when many would have been tempted to dust of the superman suit to ride the global brand story bears testimony to Richard's clear vision of the essential drivers of a business that wants to be successful in the longer term. His beliefs expressed in the presentation slide shown in Figure 5 echo those of Bill Pendergast, doing the 'right things right'.

There is no substitute for ensuring that you deliver appropriate quality goods and service. The key word is appropriate. In other words you need to deliver what you promised. If the promise is greater than the reality then your reputation will reflect that. If you deliver more than you promise then of course expect to be appropriately awarded. But, of course,

Figure 5 Performance – Reputation – Loyalty
(Reproduced with the permission of *Fujitsu Services*)

going too far along this track may well lead you into cost and profitability problems. However, an unswerving attention to the customer's needs and dealing with them with manners and empathy should not entail too significant demands on your expense budget.

No amount of communications skills, training, PR or advertising can recover you from a bad reputation that is based on consistently under-whelming your customers. Reputation management is about making sure your know about it before it becomes terminal. It is about ensuring your reputation is not an undeserved handicap. It cannot show you how to turn a pig's ear into a silk purse. In the end as Richard Christou explained in his presentation, 'Performance equals reputation and if you do the right things right finally equals (customer) loyalty'.

Renewing executive commitment

The most successful projects work through a programme of workshops and meetings to review and agree actions based on the research findings. The first of these is with the executive team. The same group you brought together to initiate the project now need to be informed as to what you have found. The outside consultant or the leader of your internal team that carried out the research has a very important role in this first workshop. This is the moment of truth for the project. You need to have the executive team accept the findings and agree to take appropriate actions based on them. It would be a mistake to rewrite the findings or tone them down if they are not wholly flattering or appropriate to your corporate ambitions. You will not do justice to the research team, the consultant or much more importantly the stakeholders who gave you their opinions. They will expect to see some positive steps as a result of their contributions. By asking the questions you have changed the status quo. You cannot ignore them and pretend nothing has happened. You now have no choice other than taking some overt actions to respond to the findings. If the stakeholders do not see any change then it would have been better not to conduct the survey in the first place. Their reaction in this case is likely to be negative and harmful to your reputation. If you feel the results are on the whole quite satisfactory and you believe no significant changes are demanded by the findings this needs to be carefully communicated particularly within your organisation.

The workshop's function is to consider the research findings and lay foundations for the actions necessary to correct the situation in the various areas identified.

The consultant or internal research team leader has two roles in this meeting. Firstly to present the findings and to answer the inevitable questions that will arise as the group tries to fully understand the responses. It is important that they do not introduce conclusions or suggested actions based on the findings. The first step is to fully hear the voices of the stakeholder groups researched and to avoid reaching conclusions at this stage.

In the second phase of the meeting the research team leader or consultant acts as a moderator. Their role is to help the group work through the issues that have been raised and agree a series of general actions that may help to address the issues revealed. They should try to ensure the discussions and suggestions for actions stay true to the findings. There may be an opportunistic tendency on the part of some of the attendees to push a pet project using the research findings as a smoke screen. This is unlikely to be a good solution for the issues revealed in the research as the pet project was developed without the research findings to guide it.

The best approach is likely to come from a blank sheet of paper. All the suggested actions should be vigorously assessed to see how much they are likely to impact the problem. Wandering off into personal agendas will be business as usual and is unlikely to trigger the necessary thinking and planning to change some of the ways you do business.

Additional work will almost certainly be required to understand how and why impressions are gained about your organisation. Touch point mapping and some conversations with the staff concerned with the particular process may be needed to understand the issues fully and the potential solutions. This meeting should lay out a rapid plan of additional actions necessary to understand the specifics. Do not wait too long to say something to your staff about what you are doing to respond to the research and build a plan of actions. Waiting until you have a complete and ready plan would probably be a mistake. If after the survey they hear nothing then they will assume the results are bad and the report is being buried.

The extent of the changes you need to make in your organisation will dictate how much time and effort you need to spend on building the 'burning platform'. Organisational change gurus use the analogy of the burning platform to describe the action of developing a motivating set of reasons to move to new organisational models, attitudes or mode of behaviour. They often quote the 'boiling a frog' story. This claims that if you place a frog in a saucepan of water and raise the temperature slowly until it boils the frog will not jump out. Allegedly it does not feel the slowly rising temperature. I cannot verify whether this is true or not!

They believe that the key to success in motivating people to change from a situation, which may have been developed over a long period of time, to another preferred organisation model is to build a no way back level of urgency. Inertia is powerful and change brings new problems and challenges to those involved. Very few organisations accept change easily. When accepted norms of behaviour or practice are challenged, phrases such as 'our culture' and 'this is how we do things' will float up like confetti in a thunderstorm. Challenging some of the core concepts of the organisation, if this is what is required, places the bearer of the message in danger of the wrath of the righteous. But many corporate failures have been the result of strong cultures that have proven inflexible and unable to change as quickly as the business environment changes around them. What used to be seen as strength is now a weakness. What used to be qualities may now be faults. But if the dinosaurs' fate is to be avoided an ability to change, and to change quickly, is essential. As Andy Grove, the CEO of Intel, stated, 'there are two sorts of organisation: the quick and the dead'.

Once this group has reached pragmatic and realistic decisions in this or subsequent meetings you can start to cascade these plans down the organisation to the next layer to put flesh on the bones and to develop the next levels of buy-in and commitment.

Building commitment from the middle management team

Depending on the size and style of organisation the process continues with a series of meetings that are designed to involve the next layer of management. During the meetings the research finding will be examined, guided by a senior member of the executive team. It would not be appropriate for the external consultant to lead this process. The senior team must show its personal commitment. The consultant can support with explanations and presentations but ownership of change has to rest with the leadership team. Nothing aids comprehension more than to be expected to present and explain a subject to your bright middle management. It gives the whole game just that little extra edge and focus. The workshops are designed to build a practical plan to implement the more general plans and objectives established by the senior team.

This is perhaps as important as the executive buy in. Many a good plan has been lost because it was badly presented, or delivered as a *fait accompli* to the people who will have to do the most to implement it. Depending on the level of change the results indicate are necessary, the time spent at the executive team level developing a 'burning platform' will now be put to the test. If the level of change in the organisation is likely to be high then it is an essential element which will ensure a sufficient level of motivation and staying power is maintained to see you through any changes.

Time focused on ensuring the burning platform is credible and understood is vital to any change project. Explaining the causal links between corporate success and reputation is the key to building a case for change. Once this management level believe it matters and they can see the realities of the current status of your corporate reputation then progress can be made.

Any negative findings are going to be implied criticism of groups and individuals. It is very important not to move too fast and that you pass completely through the denial phase into acceptance before you start to implement change. The first reaction of most people when faced with criticism is to deny it or blame someone else. Different people need different amounts of time and effort before they can accept that the comments or criticism may be valid. You may need to explain to your staff:

- That your stakeholders consider them to be arrogant and not very good at listening to their needs.
- Or the sales and service groups seem to be in dispute with each other with the customer caught in the middle.
- Maybe you need to change the way you explain and describe your corporate objectives – no longer a global technology leader but perhaps to a focused specialist in a niche sector.
- Maybe your poor issue management is a problem.

These issues will demand very significant organisational and attitude changes. Whatever the level of change demanded, we need to arrive at a point where they understand and accept that the research has revealed what the stakeholders think about your organisation. They need to be reconciled with statements like:

- 'This may not be fair but this is not the issue. The research findings show what they really think.'
- 'We need to be sure we understand why they think this way.'
- 'What has been the behaviour and processes that has given them this impression?'

Failing to reach a state of acceptance of the research findings may leave many with a feeling of rejection for the whole process. This would not be a good position from which to implement necessary change.

The importance of setting realistic expectations

Once the plan is made and the sign-offs obtained how will we announce and deploy it? That in part depends on the organisation's nature and maturity. Raising high expectations that cannot be fulfilled is the quickest way to lower your reputation with the stakeholder groups it affects. The best example to set to motivate change is *to change*. Senior executives need to show they have understood and accepted the research messages. Their example will be key to a successful outcome. It is better to promise less and deliver more rather than vice versa. Human psychology punishes those who let us down by over promising but failing to deliver what we expected. We are usually however impressed by people who do what they say they will do and deliver even more. Mature people and organisations understand this. Weak and insecure companies often do not.

The lovable rogue type who is charming and promises a great deal which you know they will never deliver can be entertaining but they rarely succeed in the long term. Respected organisations cannot rely on this to see them through. Like the 'with one bound he was free' approach to branding some organisations hope that by saying it, it will become true. They hope by writing a new three-line corporate mission statement they can change the realities of the organisation and its perception overnight. Rarely is this the case except, perhaps, within the pages of personal motivational gurus' books. They often fail to see the linkage between perception or reputation and the reality of the organisation. Reality drives perception and reputation. You can only achieve minor cosmetic changes to perception without actually changing your reality.

Take a balanced and pragmatic approach to your change projects. Do not expect to make changes fast, especially in Europe where the more consensus seeking workforces want to feel they have time to understand and agree. In companies with dominant senior management staff tend to seek to move in sync with the current hot issue and compete to show how much more committed to the new religion they are compared to their peers. This is symptomatic of a group of people who have been rewarded to say the right things rather than to achieve the right results. They may raise the hype level quickly and unrealistically thus ensuring that genuine change is unlikely to happen. If you have this type of flotilla organisation try to ensure it keeps its over enthusiasm in check this time.

Equally, if you have a depressed organisation, telling them to pull themselves together will be unlikely to succeed. Patient, persistent consistent and confirmed change will yield results.

9 *Managing the Industry Analysts*

Industry analysts observe the industry in which they specialise gathering data, news and information from you and then they sell it back to you in the form of programmes and reports. Their programmes usually entail topical updates, best practice studies and access to them for advice and information. They usually also carry out relevant research, such as market sizing and trends, that contributes materially to an understanding of their focus industry sector. The market data they collect and publish are highly respected data sources in many cases. Bear in mind, though, that this is not always true in the area of services where the amount of inter-company sub-contracting makes gathering accurate market data very difficult.

Industry analysts have extensive contacts with companies playing in their sector. They should know what your competition is doing and of course what you are doing. Many of them are both highly influential and intelligent observers of the industry whose views are worth considering carefully.

Data from a 2001 survey of 200 chief information officers conducted by *Darwin* magazine indicates the influence the IT industry analysts have in the US.

The most common use of IT market research sourced from industry analysts organisations among the IT executives surveyed was to educate themselves or their staff on a technology or a certain topic (67%). 55% of respondents indicated that they used market research to make a technology purchase decision and 42% used IT market research to compare their organisation's metrics to industry averages. 40% relied on IT market research to make a vendor decision while 29% used it to make a technology integrator decision. 27% said they relied on IT market research to determine the strategic direction of their organisation's IT. On average, companies included in our survey spent $552,000 on IT market research in 2000.

(Reprinted through the courtesy of darwinmag.com. © Copyright)

Gerry Davies of Tiger Lily, a specialist analyst relation's management organisation, stated, 'Industry analysts are key influencers in the selection of vendors by corporate buyers. They thus need to be cultivated in the right way – by ensuring that they know and understand your company will increase your bidding opportunities'.

Who are they?

Analysts are motivated to be the best informed, most knowledgeable and influential people in their industry sector. Their egos are flattered and industry knowledge is enhanced by having access to senior executives, so a brief meeting with your Chairman or CEO will repay itself in status points for the analyst. However it is wise to ensure your CEO or Chairman is briefed fully before the meeting: a young, bright and ambitious analyst who asks well informed and probing questions can set your relationship back not advance it if the CEO is not prepared fully.

Analysts would like you to buy their reports and be a part of their programmes. An analyst is usually measured on the revenues generated by their programmes, reports and any consulting activity. Of these sources their programmes and reports rank highest because of the leverage factor, written once and sold to many. While the programmes and reports can be expensive it is well worth looking to see if it could give you valuable insights into your market sector. But do not assume simply buying reports will ensure you gain coverage and a favourable reputation with an analyst.

Analysts like to be invited to speak at conferences and seminars and be seen as industry gurus. You could invite an analyst to speak at an event you might be holding. This provides quality time for you to brief them about your organisation and the opportunity to treat them as you would a very special customer. This briefing time also helps you to develop a personal relationship with the analyst. This type of activity normally attracts a fee from the analyst.

If you are having strategy building or market review meetings, inviting them in to give input will give you value and it will enhance their vision of themselves as trusted advisors. Obviously you want to ensure it is managed carefully and they are not allowed to see internal differences, weaknesses or confidential material. They have not signed the official secrets act and many will not sign non-disclosure agreements. The secret stuff is best kept this way.

They also want to have insights into the business. If you are a technology based company or you are leading the way in product or service development, lifting the veil a little and allowing them to talk with some of your technocrats can allow them to build a higher level of respect for your organisation. Their pay off is, of course, to enhance their knowledge and understanding of the sector.

They want information from you on new contract wins, news on organisational changes, etc. This provides a knowledge base and means that they are up to date with industry news and gossip. But they receive a lot of this type of information so it should be short and tailored to gain attention. Over use of email information bulletins may build a picture of your organisation as pushy and insensitive. Talk to them when you have something relevant to say. One of the more interesting aspects of meeting the analysts is the opportunity to catch up with industry news and gossip you may not be aware of. Many analysts believe that this aspect of their role is the most attractive to their client organisations and I would probably agree with them.

Reactive plan

During your stakeholder mapping session you will have identified the companies and analysts who you believe most impact your reputation. Some of them may have already been interviewed and their opinions known. It is best to select the most influential group and build a specific contact plan.

But first you need to decide who will lead the relationship from your side. Analysts are not journalists. They want in-depth information and knowledgeable people in front of them. You cannot lump them together with the media and having your PR person or your external PR organisation manage analysts will probably fail. PR practitioners have a different view of success and are used to developing different types of information for the media. PR is driven by coverage quantity and quality. They are used to selecting newsworthy material and are experts at finding the right angles from which to pitch information.

Analysts want to have a more intrusive relationship. They want to understand your organisation, markets, competencies and to meet your key executive team. You should select someone, probably from your marketing group, who has the knowledge and personal skills to develop a relationship with the key analysts. They should share common interest and language. But be careful and select someone with the skills to subtly sell to this group. They need to manage the relationship in the same way you would a major customer. They need to research and understand their analysts. They need to be available to respond to their requests for information quickly. Everyone in the organisation who might be contacted by the analyst should understand they must automatically redirect enquiries and requests for information to the analyst relation's manager. This is no different from how you would handle the media via your PR manager or external consultants.

This tight discipline ensure figures and other data provided to the analyst are consistent and correct. It ensures that explanations of market strategy and offers are also consistent. The delivery of a responsive and knowledgeable service goes a long way to building a reputation as a well run and managed organisation, but this is only reactive so far and not proactive.

Proactive planning

You need to build an account plan for each analyst organisation. You could however hire a specialist outside organisation to do this work for you. A number of companies are starting to provide this service. But managing analysts is no more challenging than managing a major customer and I hope this is a core skill of your organisation.

The heart of the plan is to identify and select the most influential analysts. You may have some data about them from your survey and you will understand what they know and feel about your organisation. Which may be nothing and nothing. Based on this data you need to select a series of actions designed to turn nothing into something. You can try a number of approach techniques.

- Invite the very key analysts in for a briefing with a promise of some time with your key executives.
- If you have a major announcement for which you will hold press briefings then consider running it around the same time as an analysts' event – but do not mix analysts and journalists in one event, they have different needs and very different styles. I have found the analysts can be very annoyed by the superficial questions of the journalists. It is best to give them the chance to attend the press conference or briefing with a promise of an in depth briefing afterwards or simply hold a separate event. You can cost effectively run two events in the same location on the same day and cover the media and analyst audiences appropriately.

- Some organisations run analyst specific events. Hewlett Packard held their 2002 event in Santa Barbara, California. They flew in over 150 Industry analysts for a three-day event. The opening session was with Carly Fiorina; the CEO, who outlined HP's strategic plans. This event came soon after HP had acquired Compaq in an $18.6 billion dollar merger. During the acquisition talks, Carly had come under a great deal of criticism from some HP shareholders and the media. This event was an excellent way to win the approval of a very knowledgeable and informed audience. After the opening session the event broke up into streams at which over fifty senior HP managers presented their product and service strategies. HP paid the flight costs and expenses of the attending analysts who came from not only the US but also from Europe and Asia Pacific. HP recognised the influence of industry analysts and were prepared to invest substantial resources in ensuring they got their message across.
- Invite analyst to attend your customer events. If you invite your customers to be your main speakers at your customer events, which many astute companies do, then the analysts are often very interested and appreciative of this approach.
- Send regular information about your organisation. But remember spamming helps nobody so the information should be specifically addressed and relevant to that individual and their specialisation.
- Invite them to contribute to planning sessions as the industry guru.
- Invite them to contribute towards marketing collateral such as white papers.

Some of the above actions will incur fees from the analysts and additional costs for their attendance but the return from this is in my experience one of the highest ROI actions you can take.

Certainly inviting the analyst to meet your organisation's management team can be rewarding on a number of levels. Puni Rajah, Vice President, Asia Pacific Software and Services Research for IDC explained. 'Many organisations find that industry analyst events, be they en masse or for a single analyst, give them an excellent opportunity to get their story straight. You have to gather the key managers together, rehearse the story, and ensure it is coherent and realistic. For many organisations this is one of the few opportunities to build a "joined up" story. And of course once you have said it, we will be watching to see if you live up to your promises.'

This approach sometimes leads to criticisms of strategy by *PowerPoint*, i.e. inventing your story only to the level of a slide presentation. But that is better than not having a coherent expression of your strategy. Trying to develop a cohesive story without the strong support of senior management can be very challenging. Each division or department believes it has its story straight but with not too much attention being paid to how it links with other groups in the organisation. Using the power of embarrassment can be powerful stuff. Drawing representatives together and exposing the inconsistencies in their stories prior to a presentation to analysts, journalists or major customers usually achieves wonders. You get the chance to be devil's advocate and can reach objectives that would have taken months of patient lobbying any other way.

I have always believed and used the power of 'inside out marketing'. One of the challenges for an internal marketing team is to be prophets in their own land. Having comments and endorsements from knowledgeable external sources such as analysts can be powerful weapons to use in your internal communications. They can give you excellent ways to enhance and support your marketing team's reputation and hence their effectiveness. But of course you must be able to persuade the analyst to say the things that are useful to you. This is achievable with application and effort, particularly if you have an organisation and story they are interested in. The same comment applies also to the media. In the same way as references and third party recommendations have a powerful influence on prospective customers, so third party references help marketing teams grow their internal stature.

Attending analyst run events will usually not gain you much opportunity to influence the analysts. It can of course be useful to hear from them their views of your industry's trends and perhaps to hear your competitors' speak. It also prepares you to be able to speak effectively at these types of events if invited. Some analyst companies run events that you can sponsor and in turn you are offered a speaking opportunity. Mostly these are in breakout sessions with a number of such sessions running at the same time. They are usually poorly attended and bad value for the price paid. If you are not going to be speaking in the plenary session I would not recommend this approach.

Your account plan for each analyst and organisation will use a mixture of the above methods to get your message across. But be subtle and do not try to sell hard. Achieve your effects by exposing the right parts of your organisation and its competencies to the analysts. Trying to misrepresent your self will usually bring a very negative reaction. The best you can hope for is to show a vision of your organisation as it is on its best day.

A very drunk colleague many years ago said something very profound – that dealing with the analysts and media was a bit like judo: the objective is not to use brute strength but to turn their own weight against them. I am not sure this explains the concept fully but it was a revelation to me at the time. Or was it the wine?

Maturity required

Choosing the right person to manage your analyst relations is the key decision. They must have a persuasive and very empathetic style; they should understand the organisation and its market numbers; they need to do their research on the targeted analysts and they must be able to manage the internal executives who will be exposed to the analysts. It is not a junior role but demands someone with experience and perhaps a little grey hair.

Once you have reached a trusting and close relationship with the analyst community they are a good source of snap opinions about issues that affect your business reputation. However they are opinions and should not be valued disproportionately highly and certainly much lower than properly conducted research. The analysts are industry watchers but very few I have met have held any significant position within a commercial organisation other than an analyst organisation. Their views sometimes tend towards the naïve. But naive is often better than the 'we tried it before and it did not work' world-weary brigade.

Organisational issues

Gerry Davies of Tiger Lily believes, 'Many companies make organisational errors when setting up their industry analyst programmes. They often throw analyst relations in with PR using internal or external resources. This rarely works well as the demands of the two audiences are very different. Typically within an organisation analysts are managed by the marketing group, public relations by corporate communications and investor analysts by the CFO. But all these groups influence each other – financial analysts regularly turn to industry analysts for market and company specific information, as do the media. But most companies do not have a coordinated plan for communicating with and managing these three key influencing stakeholders. They are each very different influencer communities that should be managed separately but ultimately within an integrated marketing plan to ensure consistent messaging and regular communication.'

One of the core fundaments of the 360° approach is to have a coordinated plan across all the stakeholder groups not just the external influencers.

10 *A Case in Point*

The principles of course are fine but does it work in practice. Let us consider a case in detail where the results seem to have proven the value of this approach.

Comunica

Comunica plc was established in 1986, and is a leading UK voice and data communications infrastructure specialist. It is based in Eastcote, Middlesex with offices in London and Stockport. Comunica provides design, implementation and project management services for a comprehensive range of communications, networking and support needs. They pride themselves on taking great care and ownership of major projects to a higher level.

Comunica's customers include Bank One, British Energy, HSBC, JP Morgan Fleming, J Walter Thompson, Merrill Lynch, Michael Page, Toyota, WH Smith News and WorldTravelDirect.com.

Comunica was established in 1986 under the name Cableship. It began as a supplier and installer of structured cabling. This is a wiring system that is installed in buildings that can be used for both voice and data. Cableship was particularly successful in the city of London in the banking community. Banks have quickly adopted this system to give them the flexibility to cost effectively provide multiple voice and data points at any desk. They can also change them quickly from one use to another or relocate the desk's occupant. This system is ideal for the large trading rooms in the city of London.

Over time Cableship's strategy was to add additional services to its portfolio. Structured cabling is a relatively inert layer over which run the intelligent voice and data networks. They decided to progressively add to their offer the design and installation of voice and data networks plus some services that keep them running on a day-to-day basis. They believed that Cableship had built a high recognition and reputation in its target market.

To prepare for the expansion of their service offer, in 2000 they created a new head brand Comunica retained Cableship for their cabling activity and created two new sub brands, Syncra and Enabler. Cableship was not felt to be an appropriate brand name for the services related to the more intelligent and complex networks they were targeting. Over six months they created the new service offers and completed a number of successful projects. But they also started to get some disturbing feedback from their sales staff and from their customers. The message was simple 'we are confused'.

Stella Christodoulou, Comunica's Associate director of marketing, realised that they needed to understand and resolve this confusion or it would damage Comunica's reputation and damage the financial performance of the organisation. She approached the three main directors for authority to launch a research programme. The key directors David Moëd (Managing director), Richard Bell (Executive director) and Rick Marshall (Executive director) agreed that they needed to know what was the status of their reputation and their brands.

Stella understood that she needed to have research that gave her a 360° view of the organisation's stakeholders. It was the only way to have a complete picture and all the necessary data on which to plan actions to reduce the confusion. She also felt that as she was responsible for branding and corporate image she was too close to the subject to be objective: 'I was not sure I could see the wood from the trees and it would be very difficult to be totally objective,' she stated. Stella approached ITSMA Europe in the form of Beverly Burgess their European Research Director.

The steps in the process were first to map out the stakeholders and to design a question set that would address these stakeholders. ITSMA have carried out a number of surveys of this type in the USA and Europe and so they were able to advise on the stakeholder mapping and how to phrase the questions to arrive at an objective assessment of the company's reputation and brand status.

Having an outside research organisation Stella felt was essential in ensuring unconscious bias did not creep in and ensuring that the results would be seen as valid and be acted upon.

Stakeholders

The key stakeholders chosen were customers and prospects, employees, partners, industry analysts. The research method was a combination of postal and email surveys, telephone and face-to-face interviews.

The feedback Stella received was enlightening. They were indeed confused. The perception of Comunica as a cabling organisation dominated the perception of the business. The feedback was almost wholly positive in terms of their reputation in this the largest sector of their business. Some examples of the individual responses they obtained from their customer interviews were:

'Cabling.'
'A cabling organisation.'
'An extremely big player – the best – in cabling.'
'I get confused which division I'm dealing with – I recommend them for cabling.'
'I don't understand 3 divisions – I'm not sure what else they offer.'
'Our views are generally positive, but there is much confusion over the divisions and range of services.'

CUSTOMERS

Customer's comments about Comunica's strengths were very encouraging.

'The best.'
'Understand logistics of tall tower.'
'Reasonable turnover, European.'
'Good project management.'
'Very detailed and precise.'
'Well organised.'
'They listen to the customer.'

'Very knowledgeable.'
'Flexible.'
'Neutral (independent).'
'Value for money.'
'Reliable.'
'Glowing references.'
'Good communications.'
'Many helpful staff.'

Comunica's perceived weaknesses were on the whole mild for an organisation involved in complex projects in a demanding environment.

'Confusion over divisions – who turns up, who you pay, etc.'
'Accounts procedures not up to scratch.'
'Communications could be better.'
'Too big and impersonal for smaller projects.'
'Some engineers seemed under qualified and not employed by Comunica.'
'Not perceived as a networking organisation.'
'Not in with decision makers for networking.'
'Not a Cisco gold partner.'

But the real acid test is the customer's comments and they were happy to have them attributed to them.

'You know that you can leave Comunica to do its bit and that the organisation will deliver.' *Bank of America*

'Comunica had a number of glowing references. I remember this specifically because we asked for a number of reference sites – we were thoroughly impressed with their high standards.' *Glencore UK*

'Comunica does seem to have mastered the art of proving that they can deliver what we require – whether in writing or in live presentations.' *Oscar Faber*

'Comunica delivers what they promise. Their quality of work is very high and their prices are fairly competitive.' *BT Syntegra*

PARTNERS

The partners were equally complimentary about Comunica's cabling skills but no less confused.

'The Mercedes of the bunch.'

'Has 3 divisions.'

'Take ownership of mistakes, can provide excellent references, professional, reliable, deliver what they promise, high quality of work and competitive prices, proactive.'

'Only interested in large jobs?'

ANALYSTS

The key industry analyst in the sector, Gartner, had not heard of Comunica despite it being one of the largest players in its sector. This was identified as an area needing urgent attention.

EMPLOYEES

It was in the results from the employees that Stella found the most enlightening. They were confused about the roles of the three divisions. A North–South divide was also revealed irrespective of division. A low level of appreciation of what the Comunica was offering to its markets and of its core strategy was also exposed.

Stella said 'I was most surprised by the finding from our staff. We had spent efforts to ensure they knew about the three divisions, their missions and what they offered. We took time in conferences etc to make the point. But obviously it was not enough. Around 80% of our staff is customer-facing so if they do not understand and appreciate what the organisation does, and where it is going, then no wonder our customers are confused!'

Remedies

After obtaining the research results the next step was to gain the buy-in of the senior management team. A meeting was arranged to present the findings to the board of directors. They gave the green light to involve a wider group of managers via a cascade of meetings. The middle management team was involved in helping to decide Comunica's response to the findings.

It was agreed that removing the confusing sub brands and consolidating the positive reputation of Comunica as the single corporate brand was the right approach. Consolidating the organisation's branding would mean that some people in the organisation would lose their old identities and the familiar Cableship brand would die after serving its purpose. Comunica consolidated their brand into one name, Comunica, with the attached strap line, 'Specialist in communications, networks and support. Taking ownership and responsibility to a new level.'

This careful consensus-building approach ensured that very little resistance was made to the radical branding approach. The good feedback to the organisation and the clear signs that the name Comunica was gaining acceptance with customers reinforced the positive feelings of the employees. The fact that they were a key part of the project was also very much appreciated. Many of the staff thanked Stella for being included in the project. Out of a total of 230 employees around 105 responded to the mailed questionnaire and a further 23 were interviewed face to face.

The research, which revealed a lack of knowledge about their organisation, its offer and strategy, was also delicately handled with the detailed findings not being released. It was explained that an 'information and training issue' was detected and that a programme was being put in place to resolve it. They knew they needed to ensure that their staff understood clearly what the organisation offered and where it was going. They instituted a programme of one-day meetings for all staff that explains the 'What' and the 'How' of the organisation and its service offer.

The bottom line

'We knew that we needed to stop the confusion and build on the many positive values our customers and partners associate with the organisation.' Stella commented. 'If we had not done this research and understood, as well as we do know now, what our brand stood for and what was the reality of our reputation with our key stakeholders, it would have cost us a lot of money and damaged our reputation in the medium term. We have caught the problem in time and now we have a clear road map of what we need to do to correct and benefit from it.'

A key quality of good management is the ability to evolve their companies rapidly to address market opportunities. Having the courage to revisit decisions made even recently, and to be blessed with the sensitivity to listen to the whispered comments and the courage to ask the big questions is what often marks out winners from the losers.

Comunica had the courage to do this. 'I think the project has been a great success. I believe we will do it again some time in the not too distant future to make sure we are still on track and gain the next set of pointers to ensure our futures', Stella explained.

11 *The Time to Take Action*

Was reading this book light entertainment or has it motivated you to go further with a reputation management project? The challenges of persuading your management team to believe in the concepts should not be underestimated. Asking the big question, 'What do you think about me?' takes a reasonable measure of self-confidence and maturity. But if you take the decision, conduct research and act on the findings you will pass through a stimulating and revealing process that will probably change significantly elements of the way your organisation operates in the future. Whether your organisation is a multinational or a local restaurant. It can work for you. Commerce has always been about doing business with people with whom you feel comfortable and you trust. Tuning in to your stakeholders' views on how comfortable you are to work with or if you are believed to be trustworthy is just common sense.

The importance of continuing and renewing the plan

If you act on the advice in this book and conduct a reputation management project, then when the research and action plan phase is completed you may end up thinking, 'I am glad that is all over. The difficult questions, the anxious wait for the results. The apprehension about what our staff would say about us, and all of this in front of an outside consultant. Well now we can relax and get on with business as usual for the next year or so.'

Wrong! Now you know where you are in the eyes of your stakeholders, but what will be your ongoing management plan? How will you measure the results of the actions you are taking and when do you intend to do the whole thing again to understand the evolution of your reputation?

Once you have the full understanding of your reputation it will become infectious to understand how it is progressing. Like watching your favourite soap opera. But this time the on screen emotional dramas could be losing or gaining your organisation opportunities every day. Your reputation is like any other of your assets: it needs regular measurement and maintenance.

Ensuring you know the level of recognition of your brand and the status of your reputation should be part of your asset management discipline. After all, once you take away the value of your assets from your current market value as an organisation then what you are left with is a financial value of your brand and reputation. We have said it before but it is worth repeating. Is that a value worth protecting?

Hopefully many positive reassessments of current practice and changes to the way you do business will have arisen out of the exercise.

- You will have created a cohesive and all embracing set of messages that describe what your organisation does and the value it brings to its stakeholders. By carrying out a 360° research study you know what you are saying to each group and how these stories interlink.
- You will have undertaken a reality check on how these messages are received and hopefully modified them to be more in line with each other, the expectations of your stakeholders and of course reality.
- You will have reviewed your sales approach to ensure you understand the process from all the angles and that your sales team is acting with the maximum effectiveness.
- Weak service delivery processes may have been exposed and for sure you will be acting to improve them.
- Your staff's understanding of your customers, their expectations and views will have been enhanced by communications and/or training.
- The industry analysts will be more aware of you and being regularly kept up to date on your activities.
- The media are now being managed with more effectiveness and you have the right crisis plans in place, just in case.
- Your corporate culture and behaviour will have been given the acid test and you will know the answer to the vital question. Are we nice people to do business with?

And all of this came from a study that costs a relatively small amount of money. It is neither expensive nor overly disruptive to find the current state of your reputation and the issues you need to resolve. But will you probably need to expend much more effort and energy to actually implement the necessary changes.

And when will you see the results? Some will arrive quickly and others much more slowly. Staff morale can improve quickly as they see a clear, credible and cohesive story that explains who they are and what value they bring to the world. They will feel much more in touch with their customers once they understand and accept what they feel about your organisation. They may have a few hurt feelings for a while, if the stakeholders interviewed had some tough things to say, but managed carefully the effects should be motivational. Customers may find the improving processes; changing attitudes and better communications give them a confidence boost very soon into the project. The industry analysts and media can equally very quickly respond positively to a more effective and sensitive management of their needs. But redressing the effects of infectious history takes time. It took time to build it and it will take time to change. It is the start of a journey not the end.

It is very tempting to try to spread the awareness that you have changed some of the ways you used to behave. If you are genuinely walking the talk and you are convinced that your new ways of working are real, not an allusion, then perhaps this is the time to give some external symbols for your stakeholders to rally around and proclaim the changed you. But remember the two examples, herding cats and the listening bank. EDS seemed to have at least tried to fix the problems and only then started to tell the world they had changed. They selected a subtle way of signalling a changed attitude with no small measure of humour. The Midland bank tried conversely to blow their trumpets before they had resolved the deficiencies in their systems. The result was decidedly negative impact on their reputation

We might think of the two approaches in the context of an alcoholic who tries to convince everybody he has finally changed for good, only to be found drunk at the next office party? Is it better to admit the problem and declare it to be work in progress?

Advice on how to start a project

If you have not acted yet but you are thinking how you should proceed then let's discuss this aspect. We know that reputation research will reveal some good and some bad news. We have seen that often the results will prompt changes in the way the organisation acts, communicates, trains staff and maybe more. So if you are going to try to implement a programme in your organisation the first step is to identify where you can obtain an appropriate level of authority and support. If you are not a member of the senior management team or do not have regular access to it. Who will you target to be your sponsor for this idea?

You need to plot a careful strategy of engagement and persuasion. It is always better to build your arguments around the realities of your own organisation. A first step would be to gather information and evidence that you may have a reputation issue. Remember the list of symptoms from the first chapter. If you believe your issues may lie in communications then gather together examples of the 'not joined up' story. Prepare evidence of financial performance such as loss of market share or information from sales teams bid loss debriefings. Then put the information in a drawer and think about it for a couple of weeks. Let it sit there and try to forget it. When you come back to it a couple of weeks later look at the data collected from disbelievers' eyes. Does the evidence stack up? Does it show we may have a problem? Of course you do have a problem by the way, the problem is you do not know the reality of your stakeholders' views.

Subtlety is not one of my strengths. In an attempt to combat this tendency one of the most effective ways I have found to promote ideas is to introduce them anecdotally into either a one-to-one meeting with the person you believe will be your sponsor or in a relevant presentation to the senior management team. I try to avoid large-scale presentations because of my tendency to want to achieve complete victory with no prisoners taken. It is perhaps more effective to drop a few very small hints and wait for the threads to be picked up. When someone bites on the idea, patience is vital. Do not strike too soon or you will lose the fish! Try to get whoever in the management team shows interest to be in the project with you. Reveal some of the evidence you have gathered but try to avoid a *fait accompli*. Involve them in the discovery process and make the preparation of any subsequent management team presentations a joint effort. Once you have a sponsor and the ear of the senior management group then let us hope they start to understand your message and its relevance to them.

Some of the reasons they may reject the idea is because they fail to recognise the role emotions and feelings have on business decisions. Or they believe you have an excellent reputation with nothing to learn. Perhaps you have similar data such as customer satisfaction research that shows high levels of satisfaction.

It is tough to persuade a management team that does not recognise the impact of emotions on their business opportunities. Particularly if you have a 'big boys don't cry' style management group. Sometimes their level of denial can even lead them to be angry if you introduce the subject of how your business is affected by the feelings or emotions of your stakeholders.

I have in mischievous moments played on this masculine denial. At service conferences I like to be a little provocative by claiming that the service industry represents the mother part of the business personality and the product side the boys with toys. You know we service people use words like care and support. I have been sheepishly approached afterwards by a number of male service executives with comments like, 'I was not too comfortable with that analogy' or less often, 'uncomfortable, but you may have a point!'

Try to select the arguments for launching this project that downplay the emotional aspects. Repressed reactions to emotions or talking about them, are not going to change in your management team. They are blighted souls and unlikely to see the light this century, so you will just have to work around it. Work more with arguments such as:

- Understanding the industry analysts better.
- Having feedback from customers about how they see your organisation in relation to your ambitions.
- Ensuring you communicate in a joined up way.
- Perhaps focus on explaining the research will help them to see the appropriateness of your reputation. Do your customers and prospects see you as fish when you are trying to be fowl?
- Customer satisfaction may be high but you may still be losing many opportunities because your reputation is not in line with your ambitions.

If the denial is not about the emotional aspect but that you know you have an excellent reputation with your customers then try to focus on the qualitative nature of how they see you. Take the angle of we do not expect big changes to emerge from this research but it can help us to tune ourselves even more closely with our stakeholders needs and aspirations. Highlight the value of your brand and reputation and emphasise that giving it a health check is only what you would do for any asset of this sort of value. Remind them of organisations who also believed the same but ran into the brick wall nevertheless.

Above all win and take no prisoners, you will not regret it once you have undertaken a reputation research project. All you have to lose is ignorance!

Web reputations

Reputation management has begun to emerge as an issue for Web developers who are trying to invent ways to allow consumers to identify the best source of information and commerce. They are trying to develop electronic means to attribute sites reputations.

The standard answer to finding credible information, product and services on the Web used to be to go to a directory. Yahoo and others used editors to build lists of the Web's best sites. But that business model was not economically viable. Yahoo and others changed to being portals with no pretence of quality reporting. Web-centric and other special interest magazines and media increasingly publish lists of their recommended sites.

Amazon, Epinions and eBay developed systems to allow users to post reviews or items for sale, and let others post comments on the quality of the people who had made the earlier postings. In effect it created a system to build reputations. Other solutions have attempted to aim at pages and sites, rather than users of a single site like Amazon or eBay. Google allegedly ranks pages by asking how many other pages link to them. In a crude way at least a measure of other Web developer's approval of the site.

Blogging software from firms like Dave Winer's Userland Software allows individuals to publish their own lists of sites and associated comments. Web reputation management is still very much work in progress. It will be interesting to see if the Web can develop a way to emulate the complex reputation system we have in the material world.

The oldest business value – reputation

Every organisation should take great care of the oldest business value, your hard won reputation. It will never be the latest business fad. It will never have the glitz behind it that the brand warriors can muster. There is no standard dictionary of reputation speak. But each new business generation needs to be reminded of the need to live by sound business values. The dot.com boom and bust was going to rewrite the rules of business. Companies wanted to show how 'fast forward' and new they were by, for example, by having an upside down logo. Framfab's rags-to-riches and back to rags story was one of many stories from this era. (Framfab is close to fast forward in Swedish.) Jonas Birgersson, the founder of Framfab, became Sweden's dot.com Messiah joining the elite at the World Economic Forum held most years in the Swiss ski resort of Davos. Framfab is still as I write just a survivor reporting losses of 29.4 million SEK (Swedish Krona) on a turnover of 195.7 million SEK for the period January to June 2002.

Companies spent millions on advertising while trying to build a brand. How many companies from this era do you remember now? The dot.com era reminded us that building a sustainable reputation takes time and you actually have to deliver something that customers and prospects value in a marketplace that actually exists.

Every generation brings a new set of managers who have found new ways to ostensibly manage business successfully. WorldCom tried by reclassifying running costs as capitalised investments. Andersen shredded their way to immortality. But in the long run it seems the only way to ensure corporate longevity is to do the right things right.

Your corporate and personal reputations are hard won and precious. They dictate to a large degree your future. You cannot change the past and the effects of infectious history but you can change the future if you start to act now!

Index

360° mapping 36
360° 45, 47, 53, 60, 82, 84, 89

Accenture 13, 23, 63
account management 30
account planning 66
advertising 6, 13, 10, 11, 14, 17, 73, 92
Agilent 42
Amazon 91
American Express 16
appropriate reputation 3
Armani 15
Arthur Andersen 1, 13
Asda 2

Barnholt, Ned 42
BBC 25
Beckwith, Harry 10, 46
bid selection and management 20
bid to win ratios 6
Birgersson, Jonas 92
Blake, Helen 13
blinded by brand 5
blogging software 91
Body Shop 2
'boiling a frog' 74
brand 3, 9, 12
brand equity 12
brand essence 12
'brand experience' 12
brand finance 14
brand studies 6
Branson, Richard 5, 43
burning platform 70, 74, 75
business-to-business 1, 3, 9, 10, 11, 14, 16
buyer's emotions 18
buying process 30

Cableship 83
Carlo De Benedetti 42
Cascio, Wayne 42
chief financial officer 7
Christodoulou, Stella 83
Christou, Richard 72
communication 40
communications platform 40
Computer Associates 33
Comunica 83

Consignia 13
consumer products 11
corporate communications group 7
Corporate Edge 2
corporate ego 62
corporate messaging 62
'corporate reputation' 1
corporate results 35
Corrado Passera 41
crisis committee 64
critical touch-points 18
customer experience 24
customer facing 32
customer relationship management 30
customer satisfaction survey 45
customer satisfaction surveys 6
customer-touch-points 65

Dan Pegg 30
Darwin Magazine 77
Dataquest 17
Davies, George 2
Davies, Gerry 77, 81
differentiators 10
Diners Club 69
dot.com 13
dyslexic 43

eBay 91
EDS 24
education 23
emotional appeal 9
emotions 10, 11, 20, 22
employment and recruitment agencies 33
Ericsson 22
executive team 35
expert panel 64
external consultants 34

face-to-face interviews 39
fact-based marketing 16
fact-based research 28
fame 9
familiarity breeds contempt 32
Fenn-Smith, Gavin 44
financial analysts 6, 7, 60, 82
financial director 37
financial performance 8

Financial Reporting Standard 10 & 11 15
Fleishman-Hillard 5
Forbes 43
Forrester 26
Fortune magazine 42
Framfab 92
Fujitsu 12, 63, 72

Gartner 26
Gemini Ernst and Young 13
Gerstner, Lou 16
Global Services 9, 12, 15, 23
Google 91
Greenspan, Alan 1
Grove, Andy 74
Gucci 10, 15

Hardman, Derek 63
Harris-Fombrun Reputation Quotient 9
health check 54
Hewlett Packard 32, 42, 80
high profile touch-points 18
Hoover 10
human relations 37
human relations team 7

IBM 9, 10, 12, 13, 15, 16, 23
IBM Global services 16
ICL 72
IDC 26, 80
incentives 46
Indra 23
industry expert 65
infectious history 11, 16, 20, 22, 23, 40, 54,
    89, 92
inside out marketing 80
Intel 74
internal power battles 30
interview technique 46
investment analysts 26, 33
ITSMA 4, 13, 17, 43, 84

joined up story 80, 90

Kao, Francesco 42

Landor 12, 13
Ledgeway Group 17
length of interviews 46
licensed to present 44
'listening' bank syndrome 69
Living Omnimedia 26
Logica 15, 16
losing market share 6
low win rates 20

McKinsey 9, 16
McLuhan, Marshall 62
managing partner relationships 32

mantras 36
marketing 7, 12, 13, 16, 28, 37, 63, 64, 81
marketing director 37
Marks & Spencer 2, 10, 37
matrix of influence 34
media 60
media bias 6
media management team 65
media relations 25
Michael G. DeGroote School of Business 5
Microsoft 15, 16
Midland Bank 14
Monday 13
most important influencers 4

Nabisco 16
new products 28
Noer, David 42

opinions about opinions 28, 31
organisational change 7
outsourced 38
Ovum 26
Ovum Holway 15

partner networks 32
partners 60
Pendergast, Bill 5, 72
Perrot, Ross 24
potential employees 33
PR 6, 12, 25, 64, 65, 73, 79, 81
PriceWaterhouseCoopers 13, 23
process mapping 67
products and services 8
PwC 9

qualities of the interviewer 39

raise awareness 6
Rajah, Puni 80
reputation institute 3
RFI 18, 19
RFP process 47
ROI 6
rules of disclosure 64
Ryanair 25

sales director 37
sales team 30, 66
Schreiber, Elliot S. 5
Schwartz, Julie 17
'selling the invisible' 10
service delivery team 37
Shakespeare, William 2
She, David 43
Skllingebo 54
snappy slogan 6
social responsibility 9
Stewart, Martha 26

stock exchange 33
Stockholm exhibition centre 21
survivor syndrome 42
SWOT analysis 66

tangible assets 3
Tesco 2
the invisible touch 46
'the listening bank' 14
The Olivetti group 41
'the punters' 23
Tiger Lily 77, 81
touch point mapping 67, 68, 69, 71
touch points 24
tuning in to your stakeholders views 88

University of Colorado 42
US news releases 64

value of an organisation's reputation 3
value of the brand 12
value proposition 6, 61, 67
Vandevelde, Luc 2, 37
Versace 10
Virgin 5, 43
vision and leadership 9

web based survey tools 33
whole company issue 13
win rate 20
working environment 9
World Economic Forum 92

Xerox 66

Yahoo 91
Young, Laurie 9, 10

If you have found this book useful you may be interested in other titles from Gower

**Practical International Data Management:
A Guide to Working with Global Names and Addresses**
Graham Rhind
0 566 08405 8

**Global Sourcebook of Address Data Management:
A Guide to Address Formats and Data in 194 Countries**
Graham Rhind
0 566 08109 1

**Qualitative Market Research:
A Practitioner's and Buyer's Guide**
Wendy Gordon and Roy Langmaid
0 566 05115 X

Gower Handbook of Marketing 4ed
ed Michael J. Thomas
0 566 07441 9

The New Integrated Direct Marketing
Mike Berry
0 566 07960 7

Interactive Marketing
Cor Molenaar
0 566 07713 2

**How to Prepare a Marketing Plan 5ed:
A Guide to Reaching the Consumer Market**
John Stapleton and Michael Thomas
0 566 07784 1

GOWER

SPIN®-Selling
Neil Rackham
0 566 07689 6

Credit Management Handbook 4ed
Burt Edwards
0 566 07904 6

Brain Sell
Tony Buzan and Richard Israel
0 566 07658 6

Account Strategy for Major Sales
Neil Rackham
0 566 02769 0

**The Management of Major Sales:
Practical Strategies**
Neil Rackham and Richard Ruff
0 566 02869 7

**Outbound Telephone Selling:
A Management Manual**
Pat Cochrane
0 566 08089 3

The Bid Manager's Handbook
David Nickson
0 566 08512 7

Using Smart Cards to Gain Market Share
Aneace Haddad
0 566 08315 9

GOWER

How to Measure Customer Satisfaction 2ed
Nigel Hill, John Brierley and Rob MacDougall
0 566 08595 X

Gower Handbook of Customer Service
Peter Murley
0 566 07688 8

**Handbook of Customer Satisfaction and Loyalty
Measurement 2ed**
Nigel Hill and Jim Alexander
0 566 08194 6

Customer Loyalty Programmes and Clubs 2ed
Stephan A. Butscher
0 566 08451 1

Measuring Customer Service Effectiveness
Sarah Cook
0 566 08538 0

Dealing with Customer Complaints
Tom Williams
0 566 07697 7

Marketing High Technology Services
Colin V. Sowter
0 566 08237 3

Benchmarking
Sylvia Codling
0 566 07926 7

GOWER

Presentation Planning and Media Relations for the Pharmaceutical Industry
John Lidstone
0 566 08536 4

Using the PC to Boost Executive Performance
Monica Seeley
0 566 08110 5

The 'How To' Guide for Managers
John Payne and Shirley Payne
0 566 07726 4

**Managerial Consulting Skills
A Practical Guide 2ed**
Charles J. Margerison
0 566 08292 6

**Creating a Thinking Organization
Groundrules for Success**
Rikki Hunt with Tony Buzan
0 566 08230 6

Guide to Internal Communication Methods
Eileen Scholes on behalf of ITEM
0 566 08217 9

Gower Handbook of Management Skills 3ed
Ed by Dorothy M. Stewart
0 566 07889 9

Proven Management Models
Sue Harding and Trevor Long
0 566 07674 8

GOWER

Join our email newsletter

Gower is widely recognized as one of the world's leading publishers on management and business practice. Its programmes range from 1000-page handbooks through practical manuals to popular paperbacks. These cover all the main functions of management: human resource development, sales and marketing, project management, finance, etc. Gower also produces training videos and activities manuals on a wide range of management skills.

As our list is constantly developing you may find it difficult to keep abreast of new titles. With this in mind we offer a free email news service, approximately once every two months, which provides a brief overview of the most recent titles and links into our catalogue, should you wish to read more or see sample pages.

To sign up to this service, send your request via email to **info@gowerpub.com**. Please put your email address in the body of the email as confirmation of your agreement to receive information in this way.

GOWER